CONVERSATIONS WITH FRANK GEHRY

CONVERSATIONS WITH
FRANK GEHRY

BARBARA ISENBERG

ALFRED A. KNOPF　NEW YORK　2009

THIS IS A BORZOI BOOK PUBLISHED BY ALFRED A. KNOPF

www.aaknopf.com

Knopf, Borzoi Books, and the colophon are registered trademarks of Random House, Inc.

Portions of the chapter "Mixing It Up with Geniuses" originally appeared in somewhat different form in Esquire.

Library of Congress Cataloging-in-Publication Data

Isenberg, Barbara (Barbara S.)

Conversations with Frank Gehry / Barbara Isenberg. — 1st ed.

p. cm.

Includes index.

ISBN 978-0-307-26800-6

1. Gehry, Frank O., 1929– — Interviews.   2. Architects — United States — Interviews.

I. Gehry, Frank O., 1929–   II. Title.

NA737.G44A35 2009

720.92 — dc22   2008047616

Manufactured in Singapore

FIRST EDITION

I never thought I was going to be who I am now. I never presumed anything.

FRANK GEHRY

CONTENTS

A few years ago, Frank Gehry was told he needed to have a brain scan, and he dutifully submitted to forty-five minutes in the cramped, claustrophobic confines of an MRI diagnostic chamber. As machines thumped and hammered, he slipped into himself and his imagination.

Afterward, the doctors had their MRI, which showed nothing unusual. Architect Gehry, on the other hand, had the preliminary design for the Louis Vuitton Foundation for Creation, a unique, glass-encased museum destined for the Bois de Boulogne in Paris. "I focused on it the whole time I was in the machine, thinking about it, fantasizing and designing it," Gehry says. "I retreat into my own world a lot when I'm driving or in an airplane, too. My father used to call me a dreamer, which he didn't mean as a compliment, and he was right. He just underestimated the power of dreaming."

Few dreamers have so captured the public's imagination as Frank Gehry, widely considered among the most important and influential architects of his time. He has won dozens of awards from the American Institute of Architects alone, the coveted Pritzker Architecture Prize, the very first Dorothy

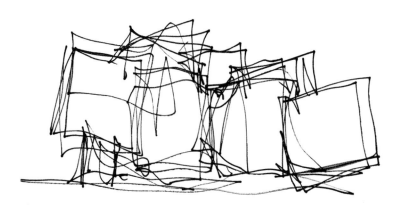

Gehry's preliminary design for the Louis Vuitton Foundation for Creation in Paris began life in an MRI diagnostic chamber.

PAPIER MACHÉ

IRVING

A Gehry drawing of a papier-mâché hobbyhorse
his father, Irving, once made

and Lillian Gish Prize, his country's National Medal of Arts, and innumerable international honors. His Guggenheim Museum in Bilbao, Spain, which led to that city's economic rebirth, has been called "the world's most celebrated new building" by *The New York Times,* while the Walt Disney Concert Hall in Los Angeles is similarly considered a visual—and acoustic—masterpiece. Projects from Las Vegas to Abu Dhabi are in design or development, under construction or preparing to open.

I've written about many of those endeavors, interviewing Gehry again and again for newspapers, magazines, and books since the 1980s. A few years ago, he asked me if I would help him organize his memories through an oral history. I was immediately drawn to the idea, having enjoyed our many earlier interviews, and what began as an oral history soon evolved into the conversations I've edited here. Since December 2004, Gehry and I have met regularly at his Los Angeles office and Santa Monica home, over restaurant breakfasts and conference room lunches. We've talked about the family he was born into and the families he created, who he wanted to be and who he became, what architects do generally and what he does specifically, always coming back to the family, cultural, and geographic forces that have shaped his aesthetic.

Most of these talks have taken place at the worktable in his studio. At the far end of the table is usually a visual inventory of work most on his mind that day: a building model he's thinking about, a product prototype, perhaps a stack of construction photographs from an ongoing development. At an early visit, the table held a lightweight white paperlike lamp, which would later be called "the Cloud." A possible wood container for the lamp appeared on the table a few weeks later, and soon came an elegant bracelet, harbinger of the Gehry Collection for Tiffany's. Another time, we took a break to look at a steel chair that wasn't quite finished; would I try sitting in it and tell him if it was comfortable?

We would sit at the near, uncluttered end of the worktable, with drawing paper and pen nearby. When Gehry talks, he draws. Our initial conversations about his childhood, for instance, were punctuated by breaks to draw such things as the papier-mâché hobbyhorses his father made, the first Toronto neighborhood he remembers, the first house he lived in as a child. His is a visual memory, and the best way to describe where he grew up or a building he admires or even a building he designed is to re-create it in a sketch, not verbally.

He draws, too, when he's on the phone, making "doodles" on pages of the lined yellow pad he uses to take notes. Some he frames and gives to his wife, Berta, as presents. Others he stuffs in a drawer; at one visit, he opened a drawer of his desk and pulled out maybe two dozen pieces of yellow lined

Gehry draws "doodles" while speaking on the phone.

paper of various sizes, looked at them almost in wonder, and remarked, "And that's just this week."

Sketchbooks follow him everywhere, including into the airplanes and hotel rooms he constantly inhabits. Gehry is almost childlike as he draws, concentrating intensely on something he so clearly enjoys. He is basically shy and occasionally seems awkward—and with large crowds, uneasy—as people rush to meet him.

He is clearly most at home at Gehry Partners' sprawling Los Angeles office complex. In a cavernous onetime industrial space, dozens of architects, designers, model makers, and other staff, mostly young, work on projects in various stages of development all over the world. The workplace is broken down by project, and as each grows or shrinks in terms of office time, so does the office space allotted to it. At one point, table after table was covered with models, photos, and plans for Atlantic Yards, his enormous redevelopment project in Brooklyn. And when design was most intense on expansion of the Philadelphia Museum of Art, models of it abounded in various scales.

Dozens of Gehry Partners employees work on projects destined for sites from Abu Dhabi to Las Vegas.

Gehry is both separate from and part of all that activity, working out of a semiprivate office with enough glass on three walls that he has an excellent view of what everyone else is doing. Windows slide open on two of those walls so he can talk with his executive assistant, Amy Achorn, on one side and his chief of staff, Meaghan Lloyd, on the other. Gehry's cell phone seems always at hand, usually just vibrating but sometimes ringing out Aaron Copland's "Fanfare for the Common Man."

Gehry Partners has moved a few times over the years, but the interior of Gehry's space seems to remain fairly constant. There are the sizable cardboard armchairs he designed decades ago, the paper-laden desk, the large worktable. Shelf, wall, and floor space is pretty much filled. Walls are covered with awards, souvenirs, and photographs of the architect with people like cellist Yo-Yo Ma, artist Robert Rauschenberg, architect Philip Johnson, and hockey legend Frank Mahovlich. Shelves overflow with objects he's made or acquired—vases, snow domes, building mockups. There are so many books that they overflow not just

Gehry at work in his studio

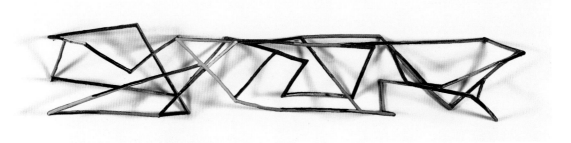

Gehry often says that artworks like longtime friend Charles Arnoldi's *Trot* (1974) have influenced his work.

from bookcases but from stacks alongside the bookcases. It is an office where you must always watch where you're going.

White-haired and blue-eyed, Gehry, who is five foot seven, is nearly always dressed in black jeans and black T-shirt. He has long been a regular at nearby Gold's Gym, exercises regularly, and usually watches what he eats. He frequently looks tired from the constant travel to meet with clients and oversee work, yet seems very fit; he sometimes appears in public with a cane, but I've never seen him use it at the office. He hosts meetings at his worktable, but is often on his feet, heading off into the big workroom to ask or answer a question, check in with colleagues, perhaps spin a building model around to see all its sides.

Gehry was born Frank Owen Goldberg on February 28, 1929, in Toronto. His father, Irving, raised in New York's Hell's Kitchen, was a boxer, truck driver, and salesman who also had an interest in drawing. His Poland-born mother, Thelma, was self-educated, returning to high school as an adult, and a violinist who introduced her son to both art and music. Leah and Samuel Caplan, his mother's parents, were extremely important to Gehry as a child, and he spent considerable time with them at their home, hardware store, and synagogue.

When his family moved to Los Angeles in 1947, the city's frontier spirit soon kindled Gehry's own. He often speaks of the visual chaos of Los Angeles at midcentury, a magical place teeming with experimentation and freedom. He told me once that had he stayed in Toronto, he would probably never have become an architect. Not only would he not have been accepted at the University of Toronto architecture school, given his interests and test-taking abilities, but he also thought the culture in Toronto would not have given him the sort of nurturing he got from the California art scene. The sort of discussion that artists were having in Los Angeles, he says, "led to my own language and made it possible. That kind of discussion wasn't happening in Toronto."

Artists accepted him when fellow architects would not, and their influence is in everything he creates, whether building or bracelet. "Artists don't accept things the way they are," says longtime friend Charles Arnoldi, a Los Angeles–based artist who has known Gehry since early in their careers. "We see infinite possibilities, and Frank was hanging around with people like us."

Arnoldi speaks of his own early tree branch constructions as appropriated from nature, while Gehry readily acknowledges having appropriated from nature and Arnoldi both. Gehry associates say they're often looking up paintings he's referred to in design discussions, and the references can be as familiar as a Matisse cutout or as obscure as a Giotto chapel ceiling in Padua, Italy. A painting by Italian Renaissance artist Giovanni Bellini was apparently an inspiration for an office complex in Düsseldorf. He may get irritated at remarks about his looking in his trash can for ideas—a notion parodied in a popular Gehry-centered episode of *The Simpsons*—but it wouldn't surprise me if he does.

"Great artists borrow and great artists steal," observes Michael Govan, director of the Los Angeles County Museum of Art. "When I'd hear artists complain that Frank had taken this or that from them, I would smile and say that's part of his genius. He has the incredible ability to absorb all kinds of ideas."

Gehry's translation of those ideas into sketches and wooden block models is crucial to his creative process. "Frank thinks through those models," says Govan, a former deputy director of the Guggenheim who worked with Gehry on Guggenheim Bilbao. "That is the artist part of it. He has a fantastic child-like curiosity that goes with the continual rearrangement of parts. In other architects' studios, you see finished models, and in his studio, you see table after table of crumpled paper, cardboard with Scotch tape, or other nothing materials."

Gehry has been known to simply walk through the office looking for objects that might be just the right size for a model in progress. Even Perrier bottles and apples have been employed in Gehry models, and I once watched Gehry and colleagues do their fussing to a tape of music from the TV show *Rawhide*.

Frank Gehry is subject and star of
The Simpsons episode "The Seven-Beer
Snitch," April 2005.

Gehry has often told me how creative buildings reflect his interactions with creative clients, and I see that back-and-forth at Gehry Partners. A sketch of his may look like a bunch of squiggles to the rest of us yet be so clear to his design partners that designer Craig Webb has even Xeroxed sketches, cut them up, and used them as templates in model making. "Sometimes Frank looks at a model I made, says I didn't get it, and tells me to make it again," says Webb. "Other times he'll just say, 'Yuck,' and walk away. It is not a highly intellectual process. It's very direct and visceral."

It's also apparently inspiring. Los Angeles–based architect Michael Maltzan, one of many Gehry-trained alumni who have since achieved consider-

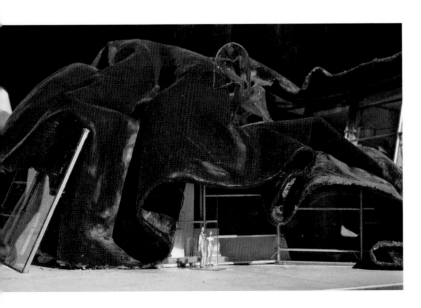

This model for an unbuilt Peter
Lewis house was made of felt,
wax, wood, foam core, and vinyl.

able success on their own, says, "Whenever I'm asked my favorite thing Frank designed, I always say it was the office. None of that work would have been possible without the culture of possibility Frank created. The most preposterous ideas were never turned away. As a mentor, Frank gave me and many other people a concrete example of what it took to make this work possible and deliver on it."

The *New Yorker* architecture critic Paul Goldberger has called Gehry "the most famous architect in the world," and few would challenge him. His face was plastered on billboards a decade ago for Apple Computer's "think different" advertisements, and more recently, filmmaker Sydney Pollack's 2006 documentary, *Sketches of Frank Gehry,* was shown on the *American Masters* PBS series, in movie theaters internationally, and appeared on DVD. That same year, Tiffany's Gehry Collection launched one of the most high-profile jewelry-marketing campaigns in memory.

When I visited Gehry once in 1990, I counted forty-four framed cover photos of him or his work on his office wall, and he is today an architecture superstar at a time when architecture itself is a superstar. Gehry and his buildings are daily fodder for publications and blogs, cited both favorably and unfavorably for his unconventional designs. He can be upset by the constant media glare, but on the whole he has healthy attitudes about fame and celebrity, probably because, like many prominent architects, he encountered them late in life. Perhaps because of his decades-long relationship with psychoanalyst Milton Wexler, who died in 2007, and whom Gehry often referred to as "the elder in my tribe," he similarly seems to deal fairly well with disappointment. He's lost

PHOTO: © SAM GEHRY, 2008

Barbara Isenberg and Frank Gehry
at Gehry Partners

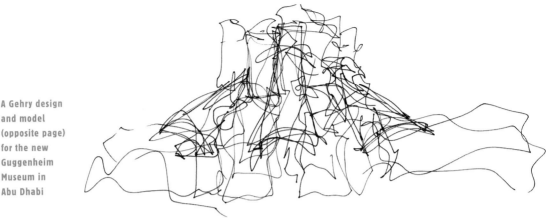

A Gehry design
and model
(opposite page)
for the new
Guggenheim
Museum in
Abu Dhabi

a few competitions, walked away from others, and even some projects he's
snared have been scaled back or disappeared entirely.

Reports of Gehry's originality and defiance of convention, not to mention
his prickliness and candor, sometimes precede him into a client's boardroom.
IAC chairman Barry Diller, for whom Gehry built a unique glass structure in
New York City, once told the *Los Angeles Times* he was expecting Gehry to be
"expensive, difficult, and ornery." When I asked Diller if that proved to be the
case, he remarked: "He's not expensive. That reputation is totally undeserved,
from my experience. He's absolutely not difficult. Ornery? Yes. Nicely, won-
derfully ornery."

Gehry has also moved from outsider to star, not always an easy journey. He
once titled a lecture "I'm Not Weird," and even Thomas Krens, longtime
director of the Solomon R. Guggenheim Foundation, says he once described
Gehry as like Peter Falk in *Columbo,* partial to rumpled clothes and with a
slightly distracted, seemingly self-effacing manner. But even then, adds Krens,
appearances could be deceptive. "With certain architects, you want to change
the shape of a doorknob and they have a crisis because you don't have confidence in their creativity," says Krens. "You tell Frank you don't like something, and he has no qualms about ripping it apart and starting it again. What
he understands is that to do it a second time and a third, he acquires knowl-

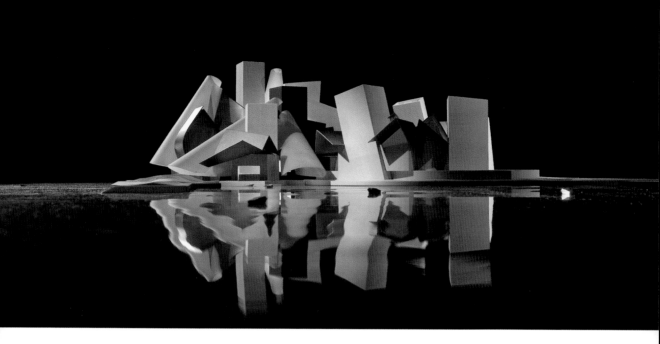

edge of the problem, and the potential solutions start to become cumulative. It gets better each time."

As I write this, another generation of Gehry buildings and developments is taking shape, including a new Guggenheim for Abu Dhabi. Writing in a blog for London's *Guardian* newspaper, Gehry described the Guggenheim Abu Dhabi as "a take on a traditional, spread-out, organic Arab village or town [with] the equivalent of streets and alleys, souk-like spaces and plazas." It will be, he promised, "an adventure."

Maybe he should have said "another adventure." Gehry's citation from the jury that awarded him the Pritzker Prize in 1989 praised his originality, experimentation, and "restless spirit," adding that the prize was not only to recognize prior achievement but also encouragement to continue "an extraordinary work in progress." Through the conversations which make up this book, I hope to guide the reader on an intimate tour of the life that shaped him, the experiments that informed him, and the consolidation of experience and imagination which fuel that work in progress.

BARBARA ISENBERG

CONVERSATIONS WITH FRANK GEHRY

DESIGNING A DREAM HOUSE

It's late on a Saturday afternoon, and the usually bustling Gehry Partners offices in Los Angeles are quiet. No one is at the front desk. Not much is going on in the huge, communal workspace. Nobody is waiting to meet with Gehry in his private studio either.

Today's activity is far more focused. Off to the side, in a spacious conference room, four young architects are circling large worktables filled with models of a very special project: Gehry's dream house. "This," he says, "is how it's done."

This is also how it's redone: Gehry's new home, a mix of small and larger pavilions destined for a half-acre parcel of land in nearby Venice, has been evolving and changing for several years now. Bedrooms move upstairs, then down. Trees are at street level and then they're not. He is as uncompromising about his own house as he is about his clients' projects.

An intense-looking Gehry is seated at the edge of the first big table, a pen-size flashlight in his hand to highlight for his design team whatever chunk of his housing compound might be under discussion. At this point, clumps of ersatz trees and shards of plastic-as-glass "top hats" adorn assorted white paper structures that resemble Chinese food takeout containers. There are power tools, wires, and scraps of colored paper on the floor.

Work continues on the house as Gehry heads back to his studio to talk.

BARBARA ISENBERG: I've been following this house for years now. It certainly illustrates how buildings don't just happen.

FRANK GEHRY: No. It goes on and on. What you're seeing in there is only the beginning of the new design of the house. In the next few weeks, we'll make

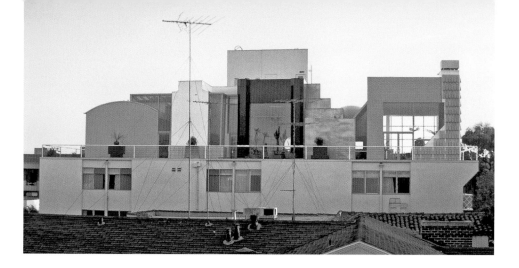

Gehry designed homes as villages, including the Winton guesthouse in Minnesota (center) and, in California, the Wosk (top) and Schnabel (bottom) houses.

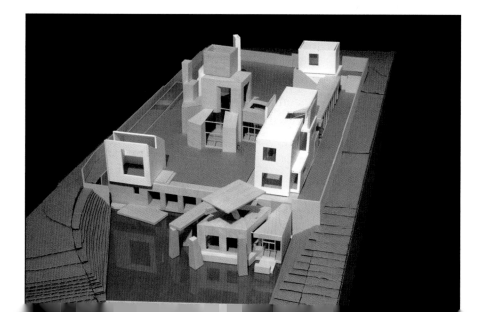

thirty or forty models of each one of those pieces. I'll just keep refining it until I get something that I really like.

Gehry plucks two oranges from the basket on his worktable and sets them in front of him. Then he moves them apart.

FG: It's placing objects together so that you make the space work. You design the objects and then you design the space between them. Nothing new. It's an old trick. I did it on the Winton guesthouse in Minnesota and on the Wosk and Schnabel residences in Los Angeles. They're metaphors for cities. I'm building little cities.

BI: Where did that notion of the house as village come from?

FG: Philip Johnson gave a lecture—God knows where or when—which was published and which I read several years ago. He talked about one-room buildings being the best buildings in history. Chartres Cathedral is a one-room building. The Pantheon. Le Corbusier's chapel at Ronchamp. It struck a chord with me that Philip was right.

An artist facing a white canvas finds a moment of truth, a pure moment of inspiration, and I was looking for an analogy in architecture. What's closest to that? It seemed to me the one-room building had the least amount of excuses to hang your hat on.

So you start making one-room buildings. For a house, you can make a bunch of them. You can make the kitchen a one-room building. The living room. The dining room. You can make the bedroom a one-room building. Now you have a village of buildings. It reminded me of a city, and the idea of being able to develop this kind of urban prototype with these one-room buildings excited me. When I discovered the pictures of [Giorgio] Morandi, I just went nuts because Morandi was drawing bottles which were essentially one-room buildings and creating villages of bottles. I liked that.

Other still-life artists did that, too. I remember [the Italian architect] Aldo Rossi was talking about [the eighteenth-century still-life painter Jean-Baptiste-Siméon] Chardin, so it was also in the air.

BI: What are the advantages of building those "villages"?

Gehry "just went nuts" for twentieth-century Italian painter Giorgio Morandi's bottle villages.

FG: You get a lot of stuff out of it. It breaks down the scale. It humanizes without resorting to decoration, so individual pieces can be very tough and industrial even. The architecture is the play between the spaces.

I used to sit at cocktail parties quietly looking at the spaces between people, and when I was much younger, I went out and photographed the spaces between buildings. It interested me that a building itself could be pretty banal, but if you juxtaposed it with something else you could create an ensemble that was more interesting. The whole *is* greater than the sum of the parts.

BI: And how about what fills those rooms?

FG: When I was doing houses, I would never commandeer the interiors with my own furniture and my own designs like Mies van der Rohe or Frank Lloyd Wright. I was the opposite. I wanted people to bring in their stuff to make it their own and interact with what I had done. It's a more open way of thinking about it.

BI: Is that the way you think about things in your own house?

FG: I do. My wife, Berta, goes out and buys crazy-looking contraptions that she puts in the house.

BI: What kind of "contraptions"?

FG: She bought a wooden chest she put in the living room, and it's the coffee table. It's the last thing in the world *I* would have bought, and it looks great. So she puts in her tchotchkes and I put in mine, and they sort of coexist. It's very comfortable. It's not overwhelming to your senses.

I think there can be an accessibility to an environment. You see it in an artist's studio, where you feel like you can throw your coat on the floor. It's not a Miesian house, where the chairs have to be exactly in line and set a certain way. For most people, that isn't possible.

I had friends who revered Mies and bought two lounge chairs and the banquette. I could never stand the formal way it was arranged, so every time I went to their house I moved everything around. Each time I did it they said, "God, that's so much more comfortable," and then the next time I was over, they'd have it back the other way because they were tyrannized by Mies. I'll bet Mies didn't really give a damn. He just happened to put it that way once, left it, and everybody thought that's what he wanted. He didn't seem to be the kind of guy who tyrannized people like that. But I don't know. I never met him. It's certainly not the way he lived himself.

I think it came out of the war, this tendency toward clearing the decks, cleaning everything up, having austerity and simplicity, making things minimal. While I liked it in sculpture—Donald Judd, Richard Serra, Carl Andre—I didn't like it in buildings. If you went into houses like that, you felt as if you had to sit a certain way. I couldn't imagine taking your jacket off and leaving it on a chair, or leaving your shoes while you got your slippers. It would just feel like you had to be more careful about things. Now people are doing it again. There's a nouveau minimalism now, and it seems more ridiculous than the first time around.

Having said that, I love Ellsworth Kelly. I love minimalism in art, I do. I just wouldn't want to live in it. I wouldn't want to subject other people to it. But maybe there's a Zen peaceful quality about it.

BI: Maybe it offers simplicity in a complicated world?

FG: Yes, but would you like to live that way?

PHOTO: STEWART TYSON

Donald Judd, untitled, 1976. 15 variations on a box. Douglas-fir plywood, ⅝ of an inch thick, each box: 5 x 5 x 3 feet. Installation view at Dia Center for the Arts, New York. Permanent Collection. Art © Judd Foundation, licensed by VAGA, New York, NY

BI: No, although the illusion of simplicity is so alluring. Maybe on vacation?

FG: I don't think I could. I tried it. I went to places like that and I just didn't feel comfortable. Look at my office. I have stuff all over the place. I like the feel of it.

BI: The office is cluttered.

FG: I like the clutter.

BI: Maybe the clutter reminds you of your grandfather's hardware store. Maybe it's comforting.

FG: It *is* comforting. I know it's time to get about 50 percent of it out of here, but it's inspiring to me.

Gehry directs my attention to the other end of the worktable. Just beyond some books and papers is a cluster of objects that includes a bowl of dying flowers, a building model, a primitive sculpture, a Tiffany vase, and an ornate red box. It is a Gehry village.

FG: A Korean group brought me that red box. The white thing is a pot I designed for Tiffany. And the stick thing my son Sam made when he was in high school. Next to it is a building model for Brooklyn that I'm working on now. All of these things were on the shelf, and I set them on the table with those white flowers.

BI: Toward a particular end?

FG: I put them together as a model to show the team I'm working with what I was doing with the house. I had them come in here, and we talked about it. Then I said, "Now go back to the house and make that happen." And that's what they're doing.

But when you talk about my house, there's also the relationship between me and Berta. We start agonizing about how we're going to live. She has one idea, and I have another. When I get it how I like it, she doesn't like it. When she gets it right for her, I don't like it. I don't have time to work on it continuously, so it's intermittent. Some of the ideas get appropriated for other projects. I come back and I see that, and I don't want to use those ideas, so I have to start over again.

It all goes back to the client, and Berta is a great client. The client has to be a partner. When it's a good partnership, there's an intellectual bonding of some kind among purpose, premise, and promise. Then the magic trick works. And it does in the end look like a magic trick, because nobody knows where it came from.

Heading back to the conference room, Gehry appears pleased with the day's progress. He holds his cell phone out in front of him to photograph this latest iteration of his house. "I can't wait to show this to Berta," he says.

PART 1 · LEARNING

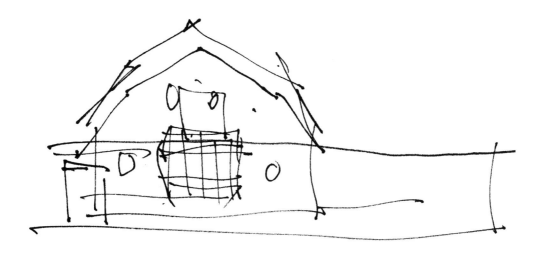

A sketch for Gehry residence in Santa Monica, California

FRANK GEHRY was interested first in art, then became excited about architecture while in college. Trained in part by University of Southern California professors who had just come back from military service in Japan, he readily acknowledges the Japanese influence on his early work. The Viennese architect Victor Gruen taught him shopping centers, office buildings, and precision. Renderings for architects during his years in the army and at Harvard brought him new experience, as did the year he spent in Paris with the André Rémondet architecture firm.

He returned to Los Angeles and opened his first architecture office there in 1962. By the time of his Danziger house two years later, he was becoming someone to be reckoned with. Artists became his colleagues, supporters, and friends. His house, his studio, and his memory are filled with images, experiences, and souvenirs of his lifelong admiration for, and friendships with, artists, including the sculptor Robert Graham in Los Angeles and Robert Rauschenberg in New York.

Although his earliest work reflects his modernist training at USC, Gehry was soon experimenting with form, idea, and materials. At school and in the field, he saw and studied buildings from such diverse architects as Harwell Hamilton Harris, Raphael Soriano, Louis Kahn, Le Corbusier, and Frank Lloyd Wright. As he became more involved with Los Angeles artists, he also designed exhibitions for the Los Angeles County Museum of Art. In 1972, he built painter Ron Davis's Malibu home. In the 1970s, he began work on art collector Norton Simon's Malibu beach guesthouse and remodeled the studios and workshops of the printmaking concern Gemini G.E.L. in West Hollywood.

Gehry, like many other artists, was exploring art made of found objects and industrial materials. His own house, a Santa Monica bungalow he reimagined in 1978, began as a laboratory for his ideas and ended up being the project that sent him careening to national attention.

Born at Toronto General Hospital, Frank Gehry (né Goldberg) spent his first seventeen years in Toronto. The Goldbergs did not prosper there. Even after they moved to Los Angeles, life remained difficult. Upon graduating high school, Gehry helped out by driving a truck and working for relatives by day, then attending community college at night.

BI: You don't come from a life of privilege. Your father grew up essentially on the streets of New York.

FG: It's only hearsay, since he didn't talk much about his childhood. I know he was born on Christmas Day 1900, the fourth of nine children, and that his parents came from Russia. His father, a tailor, died when he was eleven years old, and his mother didn't have any money. The kids had to go to work, so they didn't get an education. As far as I can determine, they lived in Hell's Kitchen, where he boxed in the Golden Gloves and some other tournaments.

Gehry's parents, Irving and Thelma Goldberg

BI: How did he get to Toronto?

FG: I haven't a clue. But he came to Toronto for something, met my mother, and they were married.

BI: Your mother had come to Toronto from Poland?

FG: Yes. She was born in Lodz, and in 1913, when she was nine, her family moved to Canada. In Lodz, my grandmother was foreman in her father's foundry, and my grandfather had a successful business delivering coal. Then he hired an assistant to help him, and the assistant, who was anti-Semitic, began giving him a hard time, stealing and trying to take customers away. When my grandfather went to the police, the police said it couldn't be true; his assistant was a "nice man" who wouldn't do such things. My grandfather realized that something was coming and managed to get his family to Holland and on a boat to Canada. Most of his relatives stayed, and thirty-three or thirty-four people were killed at various camps during the Holocaust. When I got to the Wailing Wall in Jerusalem the first time, I just burst into tears, the feeling was so powerful.

BI: How would you describe your relationship with your maternal grandparents, Leah and Samuel Caplan? They were such important figures for you as a child.

FG: They lived in a tiny row house just thirty minutes by bicycle from our house, and sometimes I'd sleep over, right between them in the crack between their two beds. They were just around the corner from my grandfather's hardware store, where I would work after school and on Saturdays. When I was old enough, I'd open the store for him on Saturday mornings when he went to shul—I guess it was okay for me to blaspheme the Sabbath, not him. We would fix clocks and toasters, and I would thread pipes and cut glass with him. We sold boxes of nails, screws, and bolts. Plates and dishes. The store was very cluttered. It was wonderful.

BI: What sorts of things would you talk about with your grandfather?

FG: He was a Talmudic scholar. We would spend summer evenings on their porch, which he called his summer resort, and he would talk with me about Talmud and the importance of asking questions. Why did the sun come up in the morning? Why did the trees turn color in the winter? Why was the sky blue? Everything was why, why, why. I think that created a pattern of curiosity which has done well for me.

BI: And your grandmother?

FG: My grandmother was kind of the community shaman. A healer. I would go with her to people's houses where someone was sick, and we'd sit and do vigil until they got better. I remember going to one relative's house where she applied suction cups to his back, then took out a quill pen and started writing on his arm.

BI: Could you see what she was writing?

FG: Prayers, I think, in Yiddish. But the room was very dark. It was lit by candle-light and very mysterious. Everyone was standing around and watching.

BI: Did you believe in what she was doing?

Gehry spent many happy times as a child with his maternal grandparents, Samuel and Leah Caplan.

FG: No, I never believed in it, but I loved her and I was fascinated. I was too young to really know whether it was right or wrong, but all the people she visited believed in it.

BI: You've spoken about so many special times with her, of building cities together on her kitchen floor.

FG: My grandparents had a wood stove, and I'd go with her to shops around the neighborhood where we'd buy burlap bags filled with small, leftover wood pieces. When we got home, she'd open one of the sacks and fill the kitchen floor with pieces of raw wood in all kinds of shapes. We'd sit on the floor together and make things out of them—cities, bridges, buildings.

When I was choosing a profession, I didn't know what I wanted to be or what to do with my life, and I remembered us making those things on the

The onetime home, in Toronto,
of Gehry's maternal grandparents

floor. I messed with chemical engineering because I had a cousin who was a role model and liked chemical engineering, and I had a friend who was going to be a radio announcer and so I tried that, too. But I was too shy. Even when I was younger, my teachers would write on my report cards that they wished I would speak out more.

I started thinking about what was the most fun I ever had in my life. What would be something useful for me to do? And I had this image of being on the floor with Grandma making things.

Years later, I realized it was a license to play. That was important to me, because when you start out in architecture, or in any of the arts, the baby steps you take are scary. By the time you get there, you've been through a school system that tries to make everything rational, mathematical, and logical and all of a sudden you're confronted with something that's emotional and intuitive. You look for anchors, and my anchor was this memory of my grandmother. That was the enabling act for me. I wish she was around so I could tell her.

My grandparents, who I adored, were my safe haven from my parents, who were more edgy. My mother wanted to be a lawyer, but because she was a woman, my grandparents wouldn't send her to college, much less law school. She didn't even graduate high school until she raised our family, but when I was a kid, she took violin lessons at the Hamburg Institute, and she used to take me to concerts. She also took me to the museum, which is now called Art

Gallery of Ontario and which is the one I'm remodeling. I was fascinated with music and I was fascinated with painting. I always liked art, and my father and I sometimes drew together.

BI: Yet I sense that your grandfather was the friendly adult teacher that your father never was.

FG: Dad, who was in the slot machine business when I was growing up, was kind of a diamond in the rough. A street kid. We didn't ever have much, but he still brought poor people home to share meals with us, and he helped my grandfather and uncle when they had financial problems. He was very generous to them, and he had a good heart. But it was very hard for me, because he was always reminding me that he thought I was a dreamer, not a businessman, and useless.

When I was in high school, my father had a lot of stress in his business, which he often would take out on me. He was losing everything, so he was coming apart. One night, when he started screaming and yelling at me about some stupid thing, he grabbed me and I hit him, something I'd never done before. Then I was scared, so I got loose and ran out of the house. I thought he was going to chase me down the street, so I ran away really fast, then hid behind a building, watching for him. When nobody came out of the house, I sort of slinked back. There were little glass windows on each side of the front door, and I peeked in and there he was lying on the floor. He had had a heart attack and passed out, and my mother was tending to him. They got him to a doctor in time, but if you think that didn't lay a trip on me . . .

BI: Did you and your father make up after that?

FG: We did, and there were no repercussions that I remember.

BI: How long after that did your family move to Los Angeles?

FG: We moved to Los Angeles in 1947, three or four months after my dad's heart attack. He was beat up, and it was at a time when they used to tell people to go to nicer climates and start over. They auctioned off his company, and I had to jump in and become grown-up all of a sudden, helping to sell

Frank Gehry in 1947

the house and dispose of everything. My dad was forty-seven years old, and he was finished. He was wiped out and demoralized.

My father's older brother and his wife were traveling to California, and my dad went with them. When he got to Los Angeles, he only had a few thousand bucks, and he found a job driving a truck for Yankee Doodle Root Beer. My mother and sister followed a few weeks later. After I finished high school in Toronto, I joined them in Los Angeles, and I got a job as a truck driver, too.

BI: What was your first impression of Los Angeles when you got off the train?

FG: It was sunny and warm. The light was brighter than I was used to. Bright, bright, bright. Like coming out of a movie theater.

BI: What was your life like in Los Angeles?

FG: Our first place in Los Angeles was a two-room apartment with ragged carpets and pull-down beds, and my sister and I traded off between the bed and the couch.

When my parents had a night off, we'd drive up to the Sunset Strip and watch movie stars. My father was very personable, and he would give the parking lot attendant a few bucks so we could stand in the front. I've seen people do that now, when I'm coming out of Spago or a party. I realize that when I was eighteen years old, I was that kid standing there, looking. One night we saw Jennifer Jones get out of a limo, and I thought how elegant she was; years later, I was doing her house, and I told her that story.

We also spent a lot of time with family. Uncle Willie was a bartender at a bar owned by Mickey Cohen, the gangster, and my uncle Harry was a barber. Aunt Beulah, who played the sax and had the first women's dance orchestra, was very helpful to my parents. My mother got a job at the Broadway department store at Hollywood and Vine, first in the candy department, then in draperies, then designing. You've got to give her credit—she just dove in and did what she had to do to support the family.

BI: So did you, didn't you?

FG: Yes, I was going to night school, but I had to work during the day. My cousin Arthur had Continental Jewelers downtown. I helped him clean jewelry and fix watches and fans, stuff I'd done with my grandfather. I'd drop my dad off at Bonnie Brae Liquor, where he worked, then take the car to the top of Bunker Hill, park, and take the [landmark funicular railway] Angels Flight to work.

BI: What was downtown like then?

FG: I loved the old Victorian houses, but I wasn't studying architecture yet. I didn't know anything.

BI: You could still like things.

Gehry took Los Angeles's fabled funicular railway Angels Flight to work in the 1950s.

FG: I did like things. It was a beautiful old neighborhood and Angels Flight was kind of thrilling. I had seen it in movies.

BI: You also had the truck driver job at this point?

FG: I was working as a truck driver at the Vineland Company, which was owned by another relative. I was getting paid seventy-five cents an hour to deliver chairs and breakfast nooks. I took wood shop in high school, so I was handy with all that stuff. I used to get there early in the morning, and when I didn't have school, we'd work late, sometimes until eight or nine in the evening, delivering those things.

Once I delivered a breakfast nook to Dale Evans and Roy Rogers and it didn't fit, so I had to fix it. I didn't finish, so I came back. I really worked hard so they'd have it ready for Christmas, and they invited me to Christmas dinner with their family. My parents were really impressed that I did that.

I also delivered a breakfast nook to the Snyder family, which is how I met my first wife, Anita Snyder. Being accepted in a family like hers was sort of everything I wanted in life. They had a tiny house, but it was beautifully furnished, and compared to my family, they were upscale. Anita was still in high school, and I started taking her out. We were married when she was eighteen, and I was twenty-two.

I was driving the truck right up until we got married. But after Anita and I got married, she worked and earned the money while I went to architecture school.

BI: Your memories of building cities with your grandmother obviously played a part in your choice of a profession. But surely there were other factors as well. Did you ever walk down the street, look at a building, and wonder how it was made? Were you attracted to architecture in any way?

FG: When I was still in high school, I went to a lecture at the University of Toronto by the Finnish architect Alvar Aalto, and I've never forgotten it. I didn't know who Aalto was, but I did register what I saw of his work. Maybe it was my northern Canadian background, which is also probably why [Finnish composer and Los Angeles Philharmonic music director] Esa-Pekka Salonen and I have a kind of bonding. I understand Esa-Pekka's music and feel a kinship to his compositions. I couldn't put it better in words, but look at Aalto's buildings; I love his Säynätsalo Town Hall.

I'm a great Aalto fan, and in 1972, when I visited his office in Finland, I asked if he had given a lecture at the University of Toronto in November 1946. They looked it up, and confirmed that he had.

BI: But it took you a while to decide on architecture as a career.

FG: I finished high school in Toronto, and when we moved to Los Angeles, I enrolled in night school at LA City College because it was free. I took art and architecture classes both. The man who taught my drafting class told me he thought I had some aptitude for it. I was so upset when I got an F in a perspective class that I took it again the next semester and got an A.

My cousin Hartley was studying at USC. He was a few years older than I, and he took me under his wing. I was still working full-time, but I signed up at USC for night and Saturday classes through their extension program. I took a design class with Keith Crown, who was a painting instructor at USC. Art history intrigued me, and I learned about all the old masters as well as modern art history.

BI: Is this when you studied ceramics with Glen Lukens? You've often mentioned how he recognized your early leanings toward architecture.

Finnish architect Alvar Aalto's town hall in Säynätsalo, Finland, is a Gehry favorite.

FG: I studied with Glen at USC extension. He was also helping to create a ceramics industry in Haiti, and I assisted him in tests of different glazes that might fit the Haitian soil. Once, I remember, the pot I put in the kiln came out so well that I said to Glen, "God, that's beautiful. It's just wonderful what can happen with the kiln and all those glazes."

Glen said, "Stop. From now on, when things like that happen, you take credit for it, because you did it. You made the pot. You put the glaze on. You put it in the kiln. You're allowed to claim credit for it, and I want you to do that."

He was trying to make me feel part of it. That was a very important lesson that resonates for me even now.

BI: You also met the architect Raphael Soriano through Lukens, didn't you?

FG: Glen was building a house in the West Adams district, near USC, and his architect was Soriano. When the house was under construction, he invited me to come to the site with him one day. There was Soriano in a black beret, black shirt, black jacket. He was a little guy, with a broken nose from some kind of accident on Rhodes when he was a kid. They were pushing steel around and he was telling people what to do. He was a bon vivant, and he and Glen were excited about everything in a way I had never seen before.

I don't know if I said anything to Glen about it, but he could see how I was responding. He called me into his office and said he'd been watching me. He suggested I sign up for a night class in architectural design. I don't know if he paid for it, but I suspect he did because I didn't have any money. At the end of the year, the design teacher recommended that four of us be skipped into second-year architecture classes. It was the first time I'd ever had any kind of victory like that. The first time somebody said nice things about me. It was a big deal when I got accepted to architecture school.

Maybe I've overromanticized Glen's involvement. I don't really know. But I do know a lightbulb went off when I saw Soriano.

BI: Did you keep up with Soriano?

FG: I did keep up with him. He lived on a houseboat in Marin County, and I would go there and visit him. I used to see everything he built.

BI: Did you also spend time looking at other buildings during that period?

FG: Around the time I was taking the ceramics class, I met a guy at USC named Arnold Schrier, who was an architect from Montreal. Arnold was doing graduate work at USC, and we started looking at buildings together on the weekends. We looked at Soriano and Rudolf Schindler and [the experimental] Case Study houses. Arnold also knew the architecture photographer Julius Shulman, so we used to go to dinner at Julius's house. I remember meeting [the architect] Craig Ellwood and his wife, the actress Gloria Henry, at dinner there. Julius was photographing buildings with Richard Neutra, too, and Arnold and I used to go out on these photo shoots with him, where he'd let us observe. I remember Neutra posing for the camera.

BI: Soriano, Schindler, Neutra, and other major architects of the time surely influenced you in some way—you were looking at them during such an impressionable time. Can you characterize what you took away about them?

FG: Well, they were role models. They were people you aspired to be like.

BI: In what ways?

FG: Schindler was interesting and accessible. I used to go to his office and talk to him and I'd meet him on job sites. He would come to USC and talk to the kids. He was a Bohemian who wore sackcloth shirts. He had a beard and mustache and flowing hair, and he was a ladies' man. He took off on Frank Lloyd Wright, then mixed it with the California wood butchery that was going on.

BI: Wood butchery?

FG: The studs and stucco buildings. He improvised on that. It was an LA thing in the end. I don't know if it had international impact. Historians could talk about that.

BI: And what impact did he have on *you*?

FG: Well, he didn't really know me. But he talked to me and he was friendly.

BI: And you listened.

FG: I did listen. And I liked the way he'd draw details on wood planks at the site for the guys. I was taken with the immediacy of it, and I thought the buildings were exciting. They were also accessible. As somebody who didn't have a lot of money, I could relate to them. They weren't precious or overly fussed on. They were just matter-of-fact, something that appeals to me still.

So that's Schindler. He was a nice counterpoint to Neutra, who was very full of himself. Neutra had a big ego and he was the reigning force in LA architecture. At the time, he had a large office, maybe thirty or forty people.

I applied for a job at Neutra's after graduation in 1954, and I'll never forget being in his office. He looked at my stuff, and he said, "Oh, this is very fresh and new and exciting. It's great. Yes, you can come work here." But when I asked about how I got paid, he said, "No, no, it's not like that. If you call so-and-so on Monday, he'll tell you what the fee is to work here." I told him I couldn't do that, and I left. I never went back. I don't mean to deprecate him—he was a very important architect—but it just didn't interest me.

BI: What about other influences, like the Los Angeles architect Harwell Hamilton Harris?

FG: I like his house on Chrysanthemum Lane, above Beverly Glen, which has a roof with big eaves that stick out with trellises on the ends.

Gehry picks up his pen and reaches for his drawing paper. He draws the Harris house from memory.

FG: Remember what it was like at USC then, when that sort of love affair with Japanese classicism was engendered for me because so many teachers were GIs returning from Japan. Teachers like Calvin Straub showed us all the classical Japanese houses which fit right in in Southern California, because it was all about wood and light. There were also many architects who were senior to me who came out of USC and were doing work that was evocative of Japan and evocative of Harwell. Harwell was kind of a king of our mountain at the time.

BI: Did you know him?

FG: Yes. I went to his studio, and it was very Japanese. It had tatami mats and stuff like that.

BI: What about the architect John Lautner, another important Southern California architect of that time who has finally been getting more attention? I understand you and Berta are key supporters of a major touring exhibition on Lautner's work, which originates in July 2008 at the Hammer Museum in Los Angeles.

FG: He worked for Frank Lloyd Wright, yet he got out from under it and became himself. Usually, once you work for Wright, you're mired in his aesthetic. John broke the mold. He came out and he didn't disparage Wright. He just took it somewhere else, and that was a good model for a young architect.

BI: How else did he influence you?

FG: He was wood and California. It was the whole aesthetic that worked here and was accessible to a young architect because you could imagine doing it. That's the key, I think.

Gehry gestures across the room to what appears to be a sculptural stack of wood blocks.

FG: See that model there, the little one? A kid four years old did that. We were working on a project for his father, and the boy was here a whole day. He wandered around the office and looked at all the blocks. Then he asked if he could have some blocks and sat on the floor, making little constructions like that. Look at that. It looks like a section of [Frank Lloyd Wright's] Robie House.

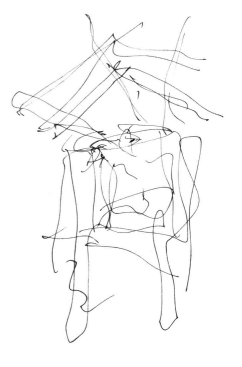

University of Southern California architecture graduate Gehry says Los Angeles architect Harwell Harris was "a king of our mountain."

Gehry now gestures to a similarly sized finished model on a shelf near the four-year-old's work.

FG: The point is that if he was looking at finished models like this one, he wouldn't be able to do it. I don't think a kid would respond to that. But a kid looks at the blocks and he knows he can do it. So he starts to do it. I think that's what the Japanese influence was for me as a student.

Having those works in wood and similar materials—they were very accessible. At the time, I might have looked at the Corbusier and other European stuff. I may have liked it. I may have been interested. But I couldn't imagine doing it,

Gehry employs wood and Los Angeles light at Disney Hall.

because you wouldn't be able to do it here and I was here. I was going to build here. I was going to start my architecture life here.

BI: You told me once that the first house you designed here, the Steeves house, looks to you like early Frank Lloyd Wright in Japan.

FG: It did. As I said, it was easy to adapt wood architecture to Southern California.

BI: Wright was clearly influential for you.

FG: I studied every section drawing, model, and building of Frank Lloyd Wright. Everything.

BI: When did you do that?

FG: In my youth. Right from day one. When I was at USC, I had [Henry-Russell Hitchcock's 1942 book,] *In the Nature of Materials*. I memorized every house and every floor plan in it. I loved Frank Lloyd Wright, and he fit into the Harwell Harris/California thing that I could access. I went to see what he

Gehry's Steeves House looks to him like early Frank Lloyd Wright in Japan.

did in Oak Park [Illinois]. I went to see Robie House. I went to see Unity Temple. I studied Taliesin East and Taliesin West [the Wright centers in Spring Green, Wisconsin, and Scottsdale, Arizona, respectively]. I studied his planning ideas at [Wright's utopian] Broadacre City and his ideas about the highrise and his Mile High Building [in Illinois]. I read everything I could about Wright's life, and I visited the buildings in Marin County that were built after his death. I *knew* Frank Lloyd Wright.

BI: What about Wright's larger-than-life persona?

FG: What I didn't like was the master-slave relationship he had with his workers. I didn't like the pomposity or the acts of grandeur with his cape and porkpie hat. I didn't like the little red cars that he gave his people. He branded his staff. Visitors paid money to go there, which offended me. It was very right-wing politics, in that sense. So when he gave a talk at USC, I didn't go to it. I knew he was going to talk about himself in that imperial, pompous way, and I wanted to know him through his work, not through his persona.

BI: So you never met him?

FG: Once, when I was driving with my family cross-country back to Los Angeles, we passed through Arizona and I wanted to see Taliesin West very much. When we got there, the red flag was up, which meant "the master is here," and that put me off. The other thing was that they asked for a dollar a person, and my wife and I had two little kids. They wanted four dollars for us to go in, and I just couldn't do it. In hindsight I'm sorry I didn't go to the lecture and I'm sorry I didn't go to Taliesin, but at that time I just couldn't.

BI: Is there a Los Angeles style of architecture?

FG: Los Angeles has an incredible light and a forgiving climate. You don't have to use double glazing, and you don't have to think about snow loads and snow conditions. The further south you go, the more open you can get. But the generation after me is working all over the world, like I am, so we've had to adapt to other climates. I had to adapt to a northern climate in Bilbao.

BI: Do you take a Los Angeles sensibility with you?

FG: It's not so contrived. You just go for the bigger picture, I think. At least I do.

BI: Do you ever think about how your professional life might have been different had you stayed in Toronto?

FG: Los Angeles is quite a different city from Toronto. The Canadian psyche is much more conservative, quieter, laid-back—or at least it was when I lived there. LA when I got here was brash, raucous, frontier. Carny business. The movies. The development was vast and rampant. Whole neighborhoods seemed to spring up instantly in desert locations. It represented a kind of openness and freedom because it was risk taking somehow. There was an edge to it. Some of it was greedy and awful, and some of it was positive and moving. But it represented a kind of energy and resourcefulness, a willingness to try things. I think if I'd stayed in Canada as an architect, I wouldn't have grown up with the sense of freedom that I got out here. There's a lot more freedom because Los Angeles doesn't have the burden of history.

PRIVATE GEHRY'S ARMY

Gehry's time in the U.S. Army, from fall 1954 to fall 1956, expands his professional experience. It is at army bases across the country that he encounters clients, deadlines, and budgets for the first time outside the cocoon of school or employer. He designs furniture, works collaboratively, and learns that good things can happen if you know the right people.

Gehry leads into the army story sideways, with a discussion of a tumor on his left knee that he's had since birth and which usually doesn't bother him.

FG: I had dual citizenship until I was twenty-one, when I chose to become a U.S. citizen, and at that time, in the early 1950s, there was a draft on. I was at USC then, finishing architecture school, and I joined the Air Force ROTC to get a deferment. My cousin Arthur was a flight instructor during World War II, and he taught me to fly in exchange for my working with him part-time.

I figured that when I graduated, I would go right into air force flight training, and I was pretty excited about it. But that didn't happen. Three months before graduation, I was informed that because of my knee, I would never be able to pass the physical for flight training and that they had discharged me from ROTC. That made me eligible for the draft, and the minute I finished school, I was drafted. I got a card saying I was 4-F, but I still had to have a physical, and the doctor who examined me was crippled. He looked at my leg and said, "Man, that's nothing compared to what I've got. They found something for me to do, and they'll find something for you to do."

They reclassified me 1-A, and within six months I was in basic training at Fort Ord, Sixth Army Division—infantry. It was October 1954, and although the Korean War was coming to an end, there was still stuff going on with those

A University of Southern California thesis drawing by 1954 architecture graduate Frank Gehry

offshore islands, so there was the threat of combat. Or at least that's what they told us. The army guys loved to play it up, especially with recruits. So there I was, washed out of the air force for a bum leg, doing push-ups and sit-ups for tough master sergeants like you see in the movies.

I would march along with my platoon on cold misty mornings, and my leg would be hurting, so I started to falter a little bit. And when I did, this big, Neanderthal-looking guy, with his sergeant's stripes and his authority, would bellow out, "Kikey, get back in line!" He called me that during drills, too, and I felt trapped in a prison of idiots who had no sense of me as a human being.

It wasn't the first time I'd confronted anti-Semitism. When I was growing up, we spent five years in Timmins, a mining town some five hundred miles north of Toronto, and I used to get beat up for killing Christ. I was the only Jewish kid at my school for a while, and the other kids picked on me. There were only thirty Jewish families in Timmins, and I found solace at the Hebrew school and the synagogue. I wasn't too much into religion, but remember my name was Goldberg still, so I had the Jewish star hanging on my neck whether I liked it or not.

BI: Your name was still Goldberg when you were in the army?

FG: No. It was Gehry. It was legally changed before I went into the army.

BI: Why the name change?

FG: Why are people so interested in the name change? Le Corbusier changed his name from Jeanneret to Corbusier. Louis Kahn changed his name from Schmuilowsky. Mies van der Rohe was something else. Ninety-nine percent of the Jews who came from Russia changed their names. It doesn't mean anything.

It was a pain because I felt that I had to explain it to everybody all the time. I like everything to be on the table, so the first five years I used to say "My name is Frank Gehry, but it used to be Goldberg."

BI: I've seen a few references to your original name being Ephraim Goldberg.

FG: My grandparents, at my bris, probably gave me the Hebrew name Ephraim. But I never heard it until much later, when my grandfather talked about it at my bar mitzvah and made a biblical reference to Ephraim.

I was born Frank Owen Goldberg. My mother gave me the middle name with the thought I could later become just Frank Owen. She told me that many times when I was a kid, because she was already thinking there could be anti-Semitism later, and she was right, of course.

We had breakfast the other day with some Arab friends, and I said, "Look, I'm an atheist. I don't believe in anything." But it's still in your DNA. You can't get rid of it. I was just interviewed by a lady from Israel and I said the same thing. I don't know that it's something you should escape or try to escape. Besides, the world doesn't let you forget that you're Jewish. Whether you like it or not, you are. Certainly Hitler proved that.

BI: When did you change your name?

FG: Nineteen fifty-four. Just before my first child was born. That was the reason. My wife, Anita, worked for a lawyer, and she was hot to get our name changed because she was pregnant with our daughter Leslie. That created a lot of pressure.

They were trying to find a name and I didn't like the idea. I was balking at the whole thing. You have to understand I was Joe Liberal. It was the time of

McCarthyism. All my pride points were with people who believed in freedom, so it was antithetical to anything I would want to do.

BI: That's why I wanted to discuss it.

FG: I learned that I was passed over for an architectural fraternity because I was a Jew. I didn't care, but it was evidence of anti-Semitism to me. Then a guy I knew came to me and said, "Change your name and we can start a partnership." That kind of stuff is what pushed my ex-wife to lobby for a name change, and why I finally gave in to it, even though I didn't like the idea. Anita also didn't want her baby to go through life with a caricature name, because *The Goldbergs* show was on radio then. My father's brothers and sisters all changed their names, too.

Anita wasn't the bad guy. She was just panicked.

BI: And the name Gehry? You've never revealed where Gehry came from.

FG: Anita and her mother, Bella Snyder, started bringing names to me. I liked that my initials were F.O.G. and I didn't want to give that up. In fact, my new boat's name is *Foggy*.

Gehry reaches across the table for my notebook. He writes out the name Goldberg. Then he writes out the name Gehry below it. Then he draws lines through letters in both names, calling out: "Down, up, up, up, down. Right? Down, up, down."

BI: So then you had your name?

FG: I was a designer, after all.

BI: Where did the name come from?

FG: It's a Swiss-German name that's like Smith in the Zurich telephone book.

BI: Which is not where Anita and her mother got it.

Frank Owen Goldberg kept his initials in designing his new name, Frank Owen Gehry.

FG: No. It's coincidental. But I don't know any more about where the name Gehry came from. They had to have a *G,* and that one sounded the best.

BI: Yet even as Private Gehry, you have a sergeant who calls you "Kikey." What did you do about it?

FG: I went to the commanding officer of my company, a lieutenant, but all he said was "Oh, he doesn't mean anything." He did, of course, and I wasn't going to let it go. As it happened, I'd stop by the service clubs like everyone else on the weekends, and I was friendly there with a couple of lawyers, professional guys like me who had been deferred while they were in school. Some of them were officers, and I told them about this sergeant. One of the lawyers said, "Don't worry about it. Give me his name," and within three days the sergeant was transferred to Alaska. When he told me he was going to Alaska, I said, "Isn't that terrible!" Oh, and I added, "I'm sure you'll find lots of kikes up there."

BI: What was the lesson you took away from that?

FG: The world is crazy, and if you learn to play within the cracks of it you can take advantage of the situation. It's like jujitsu, where the guy comes running at you full bore, and if you just know what to do at that moment, with very little effort you can throw him over your shoulder. There's leverage if you want to use it. If that guy hadn't called me a "kike," I would never have done anything like that, but I didn't know how else to get back at him. When the opportunity presented itself, I was ready.

It also shows you that intelligence can prevail. Here was a whole bunch of smart kids who were in a position to do something. I imagine things like this happened throughout the services at that time, and I suspect it went both ways. I suspect that if the guy who called me "Kikey" had any power, he could have gotten me transferred to Ethiopia.

BI: But you stayed in the infantry, even with that knee of yours?

FG: Well, my leg started heating up. It was especially bad when we had to go on twenty-mile hikes with full packs. The army boots came up high, close to the knee, and the tumor would swell. It scared me, and I went to the infirmary at the base. They got me to an orthopedist, who examined my leg. When he saw how it swelled right at the edge of the boot, he said I shouldn't wear those boots anymore and sent me back to my company with a slip that read "This enlisted man is not to wear boots. Must only wear low quarters"—what they called regular shoes. There was an army regulation that you had to wear boots for KP or guard duty, so I couldn't do either one, which left them with very little to assign me to do. They let me do some designs, move furniture around, make suggestions for the dayrooms.

I spent the second half of basic training at clerk-typist school, and then, since I was an architect, I was sent off to an engineering line company at Fort Benning, Georgia. We were the guys who would go out and measure bridges and roads, usually in advance of the troops, and it was very dangerous work. At this point, the Third Infantry Division was preparing to go on maneuvers in the swamps of Louisiana. It was called Operation Sagebrush, and they were developing a new attack mode for the kind of warfare they thought they were going to have. My job was clerk-secretary to the captain, but I wasn't very good at it. So one day the captain called me in and asked me what else I could do. I said, "I'm trained as an architect. If you want to build stuff, I could get excited about it." But that wasn't what he had in mind. "Can you make signs?" he asked me. "Can you letter?" I said I could. So he said, "Well, here's a sign we need: 'Don't put paper in the urinal.' "

I said, "Okay, I'll have it for you tomorrow." He said, "No, take your time.

I want it done really well. Take two weeks." Well, two weeks is a lot of time to make that kind of sign. So I start embellishing it, doing big graphic things and swirls and whatever other tricks I knew at that point. They weren't very sophisticated, but I had elaborate script—I could have been illuminating manuscripts for the Catholic Church. When I gave him the signs two weeks later, he looked at them and said, "Oh, those are beautiful." My signs went up in all the latrines, so I could walk in proudly and see my handiwork.

BI: Did he give you more assignments?

FG: He did give me more things like that to do. I thought it was hilarious. Then one day he called me in and said he'd recommended me to do charts and lettering for Operation Sagebrush. The general who interviewed me said I'd be working for not just him but for the post's commander general, the guy in charge of the whole camp. I was impressed. "What you'll be working on is top secret," he told me. "Do you have a security clearance?" I said, "I actually don't." He replied, "Well, you're a good patriotic kid, aren't you?" And I said, "Yup." And he asked, "Do you have any things in your record that I should know about?" And I said, "Nope." He then said, "Okay, I'm not going to check into your background. I'm going to give you a field top security clearance." Now while I was in school I was involved with a lot of lefty organizations, but I was a really patriotic dumbo and I said, "You don't have to worry about a thing," which he didn't. Then he paused and said, "Don't disappoint me."

It really was top secret. Another guy and I worked on our charts in a building that had no windows. Most of the time, they'd leave us alone to work, and then the generals would come look at the charts and talk about them. I understood what was going on, and given what little I knew about army tactics, I thought it was quite innovative, so I was kind of gung ho about it.

BI: What about that knee? Isn't it damp and humid in Georgia?

FG: Well, my leg kept giving me trouble. It would throb, with an arthritic-like pain. The infirmary was right next door to where we made our charts, so I went in a couple of times for heat treatments. The doctor would put a heating lamp on it for a while, the pain would go away, and I'd go back to work. I did this a couple of times and started talking to the doctor, who was a guy

GENERAL'S
FIELD LATRINE

Private Gehry cites the influence of Frank Lloyd Wright in his wooden latrine design.

about my age from Montgomery, Alabama. He was just three months from discharge, and he was planning to go home and open a little medical clinic. When he heard I was an architect, he started talking to me about his clinic and asking me for advice on designing it. I would make drawings for him, and he really got into it—sometimes he would even call me up and say he thought I needed a treatment. I'd go over there, he'd put the heating lamp on me, and then for two hours he'd pick my brain. He was a nice guy, and it was a nice break so I didn't care.

BI: Given the circumstances, would you call him your first private client?

FG: That's right. My first private client. But he didn't pay me anything. He just gave me heat treatments.

BI: What else were you doing then?

FG: During that time, the general also came by with other design tasks. He wanted some knockdown field furniture, so I started designing folding chairs and tables. They also needed a field latrine for the general. Since I was into Frank Lloyd Wright at the time, I designed a wooden latrine, then put a canopy over it. Meanwhile, it's now six weeks from maneuvers and the fear gossip starts, the "Oh God, wait till you see where we're going" gossip. The buzz was all about going through swamps and about the cottonmouth snakes that lived in the swamp. None of us was looking forward to it, I can tell you that.

Then I meet another soldier who's a landscape architect, trained at Harvard, who had found himself a cushy job on the post working for the same generals doing their gardens. He hears that there's a call from Third Army headquarters in Atlanta for enlisted men who have experience as decorators because the commanding general wants to go into a massive dayroom/service club/post-theater remodeling campaign.

I went to Atlanta to follow up on it, and the major in charge kept saying they wanted an interior decorator, not an architect. I tell him I can do what he wants, and he said I'd have to show him I could do it. "Here's our plan for a dayroom," he told me. "Go home, design it, and bring it back to me next week because we're in a hurry." So that's what I did. I went back and designed the whole thing, working until three or four in the morning every night. I built a model and furniture, and when I went back with it, he really loved it. Then he asked which company I was in, and when I told him, he looked crest-

Gehry at work in Georgia in 1955

fallen. "Oh God, we'll never get you," he said. "We can't get people who are going on Sagebrush. It's a lock. I'll put in a request, but chances aren't very good."

BI: You must have been very disappointed after all that effort.

FG: I was disappointed, of course, but I didn't know what to do. If you go to the generals and ask for something, they usually go the other way. It looks like you're trying to get a softer position, and people in control don't like that. So I didn't do anything. I just went back to the camp and waited. A couple of weeks pass, and the general in charge calls me into his office. "Private Gehry, I want to tell you something," he says. "You're the sort of soldier that I like. You've never complained about that leg of yours, but I happen to know from the doctor in the infirmary that you're in there all the time getting heat treatments. The doctor told me that no way can you go on Operation Sagebrush, so this request from Third Army came in and I'm going to transfer you out there. I wish you good luck."

BI: What happened next?

FG: I was transferred to Atlanta, where the army found two other people to work with me. Soon one of the generals there told his people that he was embarking on this program to redesign the dayrooms and he'd found some professionals in the army to do it. He also said that although we were just enlisted men—privates and PFCs—as far as the dayrooms were concerned, we were wearing three stars. The army sent us in a private plane to Fort Jackson, South Carolina, to inspect dayrooms, and the guys there were all saluting us, even though we were just PFCs.

We measured everything, then went back to the barracks and started designing. The first camp they gave us to do was Fort Bragg, North Carolina, where they wanted us to give them three models. Each of us would be designing one.

BI: Which would, essentially, make this your first competition?

FG: It wasn't a real architectural competition like the ones I wound up doing later, but they did want three different designs and said they'd pick what they liked. Mine looked a lot like Frank Lloyd Wright, with too much design, and they didn't choose it. Like everybody who starts out, I threw everything in and overdid it. At the end, the three of us got together and morphed our designs into one, and it wound up being a pretty good collaboration.

We built a lot of stuff: at Fort Campbell in Kentucky, Fort Bragg in North Carolina, Fort Gordon in Georgia. There were nine camps, and the three of us had our own professional architects' office, with drawing tables and all the equipment to design and make models. Fort Bragg is in Fayetteville, a center for furniture manufacturers, and we had meetings with furniture makers.

In Atlanta, where I was living with my family, there was a construction company called A. R. Abrams, and one of the sons, Edward Abrams, and I became friends. Eddie and his wife were involved in the art museum and symphony, and he introduced me to the arts there. Eddie actually taught me about the finer things in life—restaurants, culture. He always had the best. It was the first time I saw that, and it did influence me. It let me see what was possible.

BI: Are there other strong memories from that time?

FG: About six weeks before I was discharged, one of our furniture suppliers came to see me in the office. I was alone with him, and he said, "You've been terrific to work with and we've done a lot of nice things together for the army. I know you don't have a lot of money and you're getting ready to discharge. Is there anything I can do to help you?" At that point, we were getting ready to give him the biggest order of the year, and although all the paperwork was done, he didn't know we'd selected him. I said, "I know you meant well, but I have to go tell the colonel what you just did, your offer to me. I'm sorry."

He was very upset, but I left the room and went in to the colonel. I told the colonel, "I think the guy genuinely wanted to be nice, but it's just not something I would ever do. I wanted you to know about it, because we're about to give him a big contract and it could look funny." The colonel thanked me for coming in and said, "We heard it all." The room was bugged, and when I asked him why, he said there was someone taking kickbacks, and they were doing a big investigation. They knew we hadn't done anything, but the room was already bugged and they just kept it that way because they didn't know how far this went or who was involved.

Afterwards, they called the furniture guy in and told him that he couldn't have the contract. I never saw him again, but I know he didn't think of it as a bribe. He was thinking of it as a gift for things that we'd already done, and how nice we'd been to him, which we had been because he had the best furniture. For me to go and report him was really hard, because I liked the man. I think the incident says something about me and my character, at that point in that place, and I'm consistently like that, even today. Not that I go ring the bell on other people, but that there's a certain level of what's right and wrong that I live by.

Meanwhile, I'd applied successfully to Harvard Graduate School of Design. The army had a program encouraging people to go back to school, so I got out three months early when I was accepted to Harvard. The only problem is that I arrived in Cambridge with a wife and two kids. It was very hard.

Because Gehry has created such distinctive work, from his chain link and plywood of the 1970s to his undulating metal and glass of recent years, people
forget he started out more traditionally. His first employer was the renowned
Viennese architect Victor Gruen, who gave Gehry the chance to learn a great deal
about shopping centers, housing, and commercial properties. While he also learned
quite a bit at the Harvard Graduate School of Design, it wasn't what he had
expected.

BI: What led you to Harvard?

FG: Two of my USC professors, the landscape architect Garrett Eckbo and
Simon Eisner, who taught city planning, knew my liberal political do-gooder
leanings, because they were like that. They also knew I wasn't interested in
doing rich guys' houses and that I would be more emotionally inclined
toward low-cost housing and planning. They urged me to apply to Harvard
Graduate School of Design and recommended that I take graduate work in
city planning.

BI: Did you actually want to study city planning at that point?

FG: I didn't know what it entailed to study city planning. My vision, and I
wasn't clear myself, was that I would do urban design like I've been doing in
Brooklyn. I thought it would be big projects, designing and planning parts of
the city, not statistics, law, and city organization and no design component. A
couple of months into it, I realized that I had made a mistake.

BI: Set the stage at this point. Wife, two kids, no money, a college plan that wasn't what you wanted . . .

FG: We arrived at Harvard in September 1956. I was still in the army, on leave, and I left everything in Atlanta with the thought that I'd find an apartment near Harvard, get my family settled, then go back for our stuff. We found a motel and then went around looking for an apartment. But it wasn't easy; we couldn't afford very much.

The Sunday night before classes started, it was chilly and rainy. My daughter Brina was still in a crib, and my daughter Leslie was only a few years old. I was desperate. I stopped in a drugstore to call Reg Isaacs, who was head of the city planning program. I said, "Professor Isaacs, this is Frank Gehry." "Oh, yes," he says, "happy to have you coming." I said, "Look, I've got a little problem. I don't have enough money to stay in a motel very much longer, and there's nobody I can turn to." At that point my parents were pretty tapped out, and I couldn't ask them for anything. Anita's parents probably would have helped, but I was Mr. Independent, so I wouldn't do that. So I asked him if there was anything the school could do to help me because if I couldn't find a place soon, I'd have to forfeit everything. You wouldn't believe his reply. He said, "Well, there's always another year."

Gehry is laughing as he tells this story.

FG: It's quite a picture. I'm talking on a phone on a drugstore wall, not even a phone booth. The kids are crying. It's raining and cold outside. But there's a lady in the drugstore who overhears me, and she referred us to some people who rented us the second floor of their house. We moved right in that night. I called Reg Isaacs and told him we were saved.

The next day, I started classes. The city planning class, the so-called design class, was run by Charlie Eliot, who was the grandson of the president of Harvard [1869–1909]. He was an administrative planner, and design was not his thing. He had us do research on how the cities and towns around Harvard were run, and then he'd give us problems to solve on structure and other things that were scintillatingly boring.

BI: You'd had some experience in urban planning at Victor Gruen's offices in Los Angeles, hadn't you?

FG: Yes. I saw urban design projects there. I knew there was a "there" there that I wanted to get to. So when our final project was to come up with a master plan for Worcester, Massachusetts, I thought I could finally do what I wanted to. I approached it like an urban design project, figuring out the ring roads and the parking and making an urban center, like I studied at Gruen's. It was very idealistic, putting pedestrians back in the center and rebuilding the core, which was dying. I could see that as the future, and it did turn out to be the future, just in the last few years. That's what I'm doing with Grand Avenue in downtown Los Angeles.

Then came the big review, when each person gets up and presents. José Luis Sert, my idol, was in the audience. Sert's urban projects, like the one in Medellín, Colombia, were well publicized, and I was yearning to do that kind of thing. He had just become dean and started an urban design section, and I thought, *He'll* understand what I'm doing.

When it was my turn to present, I was nervous as hell. I wasn't very polished in making presentations at that time, and I was probably shaking a little bit. I just got going when Charlie Eliot stops me and says, "Mr. Gehry, you have completely ignored the problem I've given you. This has nothing to do with this class. Would you please stop? Let's go on to the next one."

I was really mad, and I was determined to let him have a piece of my mind. Eliot's office was up a ship's-ladder-style staircase, and after class, I saw him go up there. I waited and then knocked on the door. When he said to come in, I opened the door, and there he was, standing at the top of the stairs. He looked like Charles Laughton in *Mutiny on the Bounty,* and I yelled at him: "You just embarrassed me in front of my classmates. In front of Sert. You have no right to do something like that."

Then I slammed the door and went over to Sert's office. I said, "Professor Sert, you saw what happened. You must realize that I worked as hard as every other student there. I had a different point of view, which I think you would understand and realize that I was in the wrong pew. I would like to transfer into urban design."

BI: What did Sert say to that?

FG: He said I'd have to go home and reapply. I told him I had a wife and two kids and no money and couldn't do that. But he said, "That's the only way. You can't just transfer like this." He was very rigid. And I held it against him forever.

I couldn't get my tuition back, and I couldn't transfer into anything I wanted. But they gave me special student status so I could audit classes to finish the year. So that's what I did.

Margaret Mead was there in anthropology and so was Ruth Benedict. J. Robert Oppenheimer came and gave six lectures, and I attended all of those. I saw Norman Thomas debate Howard Fast.

Jacqueline Tyrwhitt, a planner who worked with Corbusier, took me under her wing because she liked Victor Gruen. I got to know a lot of kids in the architecture school, so I was able to sit in on their lectures and classes, too. The architect Paul Rudolph was there, and he would come in late at night, sometimes midnight, and give "crits" until two in the morning, and so I used to follow him around. Walter Gropius was there.

I didn't think so when it was happening, but I did really use the time well. This was a time of enlightenment politically, and it got me very involved with political processes. I didn't need the degree; I already had one. Years later, they gave me an honorary degree.

BI: What did you learn there about Le Corbusier?

FG: Sert was a great fan of Corb's, so Corb was very present in the culture. He wasn't there, but Sert brought many Corb people to Harvard during the time I was there. Corb had sent his associate Jacques Michelet to Harvard's master class, so my friends and I spent time with him. My French friend Mark Biass trained in France, and Corb was his hero, so all the talk was about Corb. We already knew what he was doing at his [Notre Dame du Haut] chapel at Ronchamp, since it was being built around the time we were at school, and it was very exciting.

BI: How would you characterize Le Corbusier's influence on you?

FG: Corb is the lightbulb. Number one on my hit parade. Before Harvard, I was so Japan- and Asia-centric, because of that emphasis at USC. This was dif-

Gehry tries to visit Le Corbusier's historic Notre Dame du Haut in Ronchamp, France, every year.

ferent from Frank Lloyd Wright and the aesthetic I was brought up on. Going to Harvard, I got put in that other world, which made it imperative for me to go to Europe, which I did. I looked at everything then. It's when I first saw work by [Spanish architect Antonio] Gaudi. I went to see all the Gaudi buildings, his Park Güell. It's where I saw the churches and all the Romanesque architecture which got to me.

BI: The first time you saw Le Corbusier's paintings was also at Harvard, wasn't it?

FG: Oh boy. That really turned me on. Le Corbusier had a show of his paintings in Robinson Hall. I was already interested in paintings at that time— I think I've always been interested. I'd taken art history at USC, and I was involved with the artists there and going to galleries. So when I saw Corb's paintings, I could relate to them and get excited because at that point I didn't know any other architects who did that.

I already was very opinionated, and I knew these weren't paintings that would be sold in New York galleries. But I was intrigued with the way you could see in the paintings that he was working out a formal language, in 2-D. I knew there was something in painting to learn from, and then I saw it actually working. It was hands-on. This guy was doing it.

It didn't excite me to paint, because by then I had a reverence for painting and knew that wasn't what I was going to do. But seeing these shapes in Corb's paintings and again in his buildings, I saw that he was developing his own language. I realized he was painting his ideas, and that was his way of getting at it. I never forgot that. And the way I translated it in the end, for myself, is to do it with my drawings.

BI: You were also working while you were at Harvard. Did that prove profitable?

Gehry is impressed with how Le Corbusier developed his own language in paintings as well as architecture.

FG: I was on the GI Bill, which paid something, but not the whole thing. I worked for a landscape architect, Hideo Sasaki, and before that I worked for the architecture office of Robert and Company, and I got to know a lot of the local architects. It's what I had done in the army, too, on weekends when I connected with the architects in Atlanta. John Portman was just starting out then, and I used to do his renderings. I did Richard Aeck's renderings. Since I was always interested in city planning, I also did some work for the architect and planner Andrew Steiner. Working for them all didn't hurt. It got my skills going.

There was an urban design conference that they used to have at Harvard, and I think that was the last thing I attended. There were architects there from all over the world, including someone from USC I knew, Jack Bevash, who was working for the big Los Angeles firm Pereira & Luckman. My fifth-year professor at USC architecture school was Bill Pereira, who was my thesis adviser and loved my work, and he apparently told Bevash to recruit me. It hadn't worked out for me to go back to Gruen's after school, which is what I assumed I would do since I loved Victor Gruen and the people there, so when Bevash came and offered me this job, I said I would take it.

BI: What made you come back to Los Angeles? Did you ever think about staying on the East Coast? Or going back to Canada?

FG: Well, my mother and father were here, and my sister was here. My wife's family was here. So we moved back and I went to work for Pereira & Luckman. I worked on the Los Angeles airport, for one thing, and there's still some residual stuff out there that I did. Nothing to brag about.

But that office didn't have the idealism that the Gruen office had, which I missed. I had lunch with Rudi Baumfeld, the design partner at Gruen, because I liked him and we were friends and so we kept in touch. I wasn't consciously looking for a job, but I learned at lunch that Gruen hoped I would come back.

BI: So you went back to Gruen?

FG: Absolutely. I ran. They talked more my language. They were doing low-cost housing, very idealistic stuff. I did really well there, and in fact I thought I was going to stay there. I started working on mixed-use projects like Midtown Plaza in Rochester, New York, which had offices, department stores, shopping. I worked on housing, because there was lots of FHA housing being done, and on a tower in Westwood [in Los Angeles] that's still there. Rudi and those guys designed the tower, but I did the planning, apartment layouts, and all the stuff inside. I coordinated the structure and the mechanical, so I was really given a lot of responsibility. And I was designing shopping centers.

BI: So many of these experiences were crucial to you later. How did you get involved with Gruen initially?

FG: The architecture dean at USC, Arthur Gallion, got me a summer job at Gruen's when I was in my third year. They liked me, and I liked them, Rudi especially. He nurtured me. He was always looking after me. I worked there every summer, and then again after I graduated college until I was drafted. After Rudi brought me back in, I stayed with them until 1960. During those three years, I was project captain for twenty or twenty-five projects. I had a lot of responsibility, and I worked day and night.

BI: Why did you leave?

FG: Well, the place was becoming corporate. It became obvious that it was more business-oriented and things the designer types like me were doing were shoved aside. You see that happen when offices grow big. And I think from their side I was becoming a little bit of a renegade, maybe a little unpredictable. Rudi had cut me loose and let me do stuff on my own. I was kind of anointed there for a while. They gave me my own office. It was small, but it was my own office, and I had use of the secretary, because I had to do a lot of correspondence. I was running the project budgets, and at least twenty people reported to me.

I became known as the housing expert. I loved doing housing. I was really good at it, and if they had a rush job, I could churn out work faster than anybody else. They promoted everybody around me to associate, which is the first step to being a partner, but they never made me an associate.

BI: Do you know why?

FG: I had a mind of my own. I was always trying to push things, and they weren't about that. Maybe I was immature.

BI: So you left.

FG: My Harvard friend Mark Biass was begging me to come to Paris. Anita, who had a pen pal in Paris, was always after me about how she wanted to go live in Paris, and it seemed like it would be a way to repay her for all the things I got to do. It was her turn. I wasn't against it, and the opportunity came up.

I was moonlighting then with Greg Walsh, my buddy from school who I got to work at Gruen's. We had just done the Steeves house in Brentwood, and my portion of the fee was sixteen hundred dollars. I found out from the Holland America Line that for twelve hundred dollars Anita and the kids and I could go to Paris, and Mark said he thought he could get me a job.

I bought the tickets, then went to the office and wrote a note saying I was going to France for a year, and I didn't want to work for them anymore anyway. I said I was going to move on, but they didn't believe it. They just gave me better work to do. They thought that would do it. But I was determined, and Anita wouldn't let me not go anyway. It was also time to go. So I left and went to Paris, where I worked at the André Rémondet architecture firm.

BI: What did you do at the Rémondet office?

FG: I was there for ten months as a designer-draftsman. I designed a commercial center for the city of Pau for a competition and we won.

BI: How did Gruen handle your departure?

FG: While I was in Paris, Victor looked me up when he was there on a visit. We had a picnic, and he told me he was going to open a Paris office and wanted me to be the head of it with him. He wanted to spend more time in Vienna and in Europe. I was earning ninety cents an hour, and all of a sudden he was offering me an American salary. I thought, What an opportunity, and within the same split second, I turned to him and said, "I can't do it." I don't know what gave me the guts to do that, but I did. I said, "I have another agenda, and I've got to stick to it. I want to be on my own. I don't know how I'm going to get there, but I have to start sometime and now is the time to start." He was very angry, because he was counting on it, and I'll never forget how he slammed the car door.

BI: Did you ever see him again?

FG: I did. Years later, when I was doing a Magnin's store, Cyril Magnin had a luncheon for the opening. Victor was at the head table, and Cyril talked about how I grew up in Victor's tutelage and had been one of his bright young designers. Victor was very solicitous, but I didn't see him again before he died. I loved him but I couldn't express it, so he probably didn't know.

I also got to be good friends with Victor's partner Edgardo Contini, and when I started my practice, Rudi and Edgardo kept in touch with me, and it continued right up until they died. They used to come to the office. Rudi was really impressed when I did the Ron Davis house. He thought I had started something. A new language, he called it. I couldn't figure out what he was talking about, but they were very supportive. They helped me get the Magnin jobs.

BI: If you were going to extract something from that Victor Gruen experience, what would it be?

FG: It gave me the confidence to go out on my own and, when the opportunity arose, to take on a multistory building. I wasn't afraid of it, because I had already done it. It wasn't a mystery to me. I understood shopping centers backwards and forwards. I knew department store people, and I knew construction. I could write contracts and letters. I could handle budgeting. I acquired all the things I needed for what I'm doing now. It was a great experience.

They must have recognized something in me that I didn't understand at the time, because they certainly gave me a lot to do. They didn't think the way I think—they thought about a building as an economic construct which you just decorated—and they wouldn't let me design the final product, but they had me do everything up to it. Rudi drew beautifully, too. I loved the way he drew, and he taught me how to detail cabinets.

BI: Yet your work was so different when you went out on your own.

FG: I say it in my lectures. I was trained by this Viennese master, and then I didn't have budgets to do work like that. I was down in the "wham, bam,

Gehry started work on
a Malibu residence for
painter Ron Davis in 1968.

thank you, ma'am" culture, with hammer marks on the wood and stuff like that. That's when I realized Rauschenberg and all these guys were doing paintings that I loved, with that aesthetic that was kind of visceral and very strong and engaging emotionally. You didn't have to get this perfection. You could go another way. When I started my own practice, that unleashed me.

BI: You sometimes refer to your home and studio for the influential graphic designer Louis Danziger as your first "big hit."

FG: Yes. In 1962, I started my practice in Los Angeles, and I had a pretty steady stream of projects. I don't know how I did it actually, when I look back. I mean, money was really scarce. And then a few years later, I started working on the Danziger house in West Hollywood.

Lou Danziger was a close friend of Frederick Usher, a legendary designer I worked with at Victor Gruen's. Lou was expanding his office and also wanted to live there. When he talked with Fred about it, Fred suggested he use me. Greg Walsh, who was working with me at the time, and I did several studies. Because Lou was well known in design circles, it was an important commission.

Before then, I was doing everything Japanese style, which was what we were doing in school. But at this point, I was very smitten with [the architect] Louis Kahn, and I would guess that had a strong influence on me.

We experimented with the plaster on the outside, which was a technique that wasn't used for buildings like this. It was a tunnel mix used in freeway design. I actually rented a stucco machine and tried it out on a building in Venice that a friend of mine let me do, just to get the stucco right, to get the right nozzle to spray the stuff out of the machine, and to get the rough texture.

The architecture writer Esther McCoy didn't like the apartment building on Highland that I'd done before the Danziger house because it was too romantic for her. It wasn't modernist enough. But this building she could relate to, and she wrote an article about it. Then *Progressive Architecture* ran it as a news item with a tiny picture.

That was my first brush with fame, and I think it did open some dialogue with the local architects. [The architect] Bernard Zimmerman didn't like it, because I fattened the wall. That way, the window was deeper set and I got a bigger shadow. It made the building more sculptural, too, instead of just a

PHOTO: © JIM McHUGH 2007

Gehry considers his 1965 Danziger studio and residence in Hollywood his first "big hit."

cracker-box building. It took it away from the tract house look, and gave it a feeling of density or substance. It made a stronger feeling. I also used industrial windows, which at that time the local architects didn't like, but it got me into a dialogue with some of these people.

BI: So other architects began paying attention. Was that the big difference after Danziger?

FG: I felt like I was more visible, yes.

BI: This is also around the time you first got involved with the Rouse Company, wasn't it?

FG: Yes. When the Rouse Company was building the new city of Columbia, Maryland, in the early 1960s, I met the guy who was the chief planner. He showed me what they were doing and asked me to be the chief architectural designer. But I had just opened my office and I didn't want to backtrack, so even though it was tempting, I turned it down. They called me the next day to say they still wanted me to design buildings and they were willing to let me design them in my own office. It was based on that that I did the Merriweather

Gehry designed many buildings in Columbia, Maryland, for the Rouse Company in the 1960s and 1970s, including the Rouse Company headquarters in 1974.

Gehry's Merriweather Post Pavilion was his first building to be reviewed in *The New York Times*.

Post Pavilion, the Reception Center, and then, subsequently, the Rouse Company headquarters and, in Santa Monica, the Santa Monica Place mall.

The Merriweather Post Pavilion [in 1967] was the first one to be reviewed in *The New York Times*.

Gehry unearths an early book on his work, finds the page that features the pavilion, and reads aloud.

FG: Here it is. Harold Schonberg, the *New York Times* music critic, called it "an unqualified architectural and acoustical success." There was a lot of rain on opening night, and he wrote that even with all that rain, it sounded good. He also said: "The shed is exceptionally handsome, with pleasing proportions, clean lines and an unobtrusive kind of finish that fits perfectly into the landscape."

BI: Do you remember how you felt when you first read that?

Gehry smiles at the memory.

FG: I had just come home from the opening and was having dinner at [the actor] Ben Gazzara's house. Ben and his wife [the actress Janice Rule] had a beach house, and we'd gone over there to spend Sunday afternoon with them. Esther Williams and Fernando Lamas were there, as were other dignitaries of the silver screen. Ben was saving the review because he was so proud of me, and he read it out loud. When he finished reading it, I swam in the pool with Esther and Fernando. I had arrived.

SHOULD AN ARTWORK HAVE TOILETS?

ew subjects interest Gehry as much as the subject of art, and few people inspire him as much as artists do. With the legendary Ferus Gallery as its focal point in the late 1950s and early 1960s, a generation of Los Angeles–based artists was making the city a vital center for art and artists both. Gehry, who opened shop himself during that period, talks again and again of those times, those artists.

In May 2005, the Gehry-designed Frederick R. Weisman Art Museum in Minneapolis presented "West! Frank Gehry and the Artists of Venice Beach, 1962–1978." The exhibition, which Gehry helped to assemble, traced the intersecting ideas and work of the architect and sixteen artists from the time Gehry opened his first office in 1962 until 1978, when Gehry successfully used his own home to test and expand his architectural ideas.

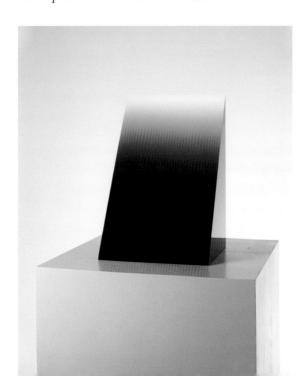

Peter Alexander, whose 1968 sculpture *Untitled (Wedge)* is shown at left, is among the Los Angeles artists who influenced Gehry.

Photos, artworks, and other mementos of those times dot both Gehry's home and his office, and the architect frequently hosts art exhibitions at his office complex.

FG: Whenever I give talks, I talk about those Los Angeles artists. That was a moment in time that was really important for me. It isn't that I was copying them, but that there was a level of inspiration. Everybody was at about the same position, including me.

BI: When did your relationships with artists start being important to you?

FG: From the beginning of my adult life, I always related more to artists than to architects. I found it easier and more exciting to be with them. When I was studying at USC, art and architecture were taught in the same building, Harris Hall, and some of the classes were in the same rooms. So the entire time I was at USC studying architecture, I was exposed to the USC art program. Because I had been a member of the art program, I kept trying to bring the two groups together. It was like they were on two different planets, and I could never figure that out. So I lived this kind of double life while I was in architecture school. Which I guess is what I continue to do.

When I finished architecture school, I liked Kahn and Corbusier and other architects, but I still felt there was something more that the artists were doing. They were pushing into a visual language, and I thought that if a visual language could apply to art, which it obviously could, it could also apply to architecture.

During my year in France, I spent a lot of time looking at Romanesque churches and Romanesque paintings, and the way they fit with the architecture. The architecture and the paintings were at peace with each other, and I've always looked for that. The only artist of our time who I found did it with success was [nineteenth-century Mexican muralist José Clemente] Orozco, and you see it in the orphanage in Guadalajara, Mexico, where Orozco's paintings hold their own with the architecture. Diego Rivera's paintings didn't play as well with the architecture. The buildings were more powerful. Orozco changed the balance—his paintings were as powerful as the architecture.

BI: There's long been discussion of art versus architecture in your work.

FG: There are some artists who are offended when you use the word "art" for a building that has toilets in it. So to support their narrow-mindedness, I avoid use of the term. But history has acknowledged that Bernini was an artist as well as an architect, and so was Michelangelo. It's possible that an architect can also be an artist.

BI: Do you think of buildings like Walt Disney Concert Hall or the Guggenheim Bilbao as sculpture or architecture? They've been called both.

FG: I'm not comfortable using the word "sculpture." I've used it before, but I don't think it's really the right word. It's a building. The words "sculpture," "art," and "architecture" are loaded, and when we use them, they have a lot of different meanings. So I'd rather just say I'm an architect.

BI: It isn't uncommon for architects to also be interested in art. You saw what Corbusier was doing with painting when you were at Harvard. When you were working for Victor Gruen, were there people who influenced you even more toward art?

FG: Yes. The designer Marion Sampler, who was in charge of graphics for Gruen, was doing some serious painting. He and I became close friends, and we would go to art galleries together for their Monday-night art walks and on weekends. Marion sort of tweaked me over into the gallery scene, and my sister [educator Doreen Nelson] was married then to an art dealer, Rolf Nelson. My friend and early mentor Fred Usher had worked with [architect and designer] Charles Eames before he worked for Gruen, and I was meeting a lot of artists through him as well.

BI: But the crucial introduction to that generation of Los Angeles artists came with the Danziger house, didn't it?

FG: Yes. When I went to the project site one day, [the artist] Ed Moses was standing there. I knew who he was when he introduced himself, and I was so excited that he was interested. He was very complimentary and brought around some of his guys, like [the artists] Ken Price and Billy Al Bengston. They would hang out at the site during construction.

Through them, I was invited into the group that hung around the Ferus Gallery: Ed Ruscha, Peter Alexander, John Altoon, Bob Irwin, Bob Graham, Larry Bell, Tony Berlant, Dennis Hopper. Then the young kids came in, Laddie Dill and Chuck Arnoldi. They were very supportive.

BI: It was a pretty solid artists' community at that time, wasn't it?

FG: Well, there was certainly a group of people who were welded together. They hung out together, dated each other's girlfriends. It was a communal scene, and every night we met somewhere. I had been divorced from Anita in 1966, and I was single then. There was always something going on. Once we put together a little band, and since I couldn't play a musical instrument, I used a bicycle handle bar and a little bell to create one. Ed played the kazoo. Larry Bell played the guitar.

I think it was all held together by John Altoon. He was like the pope of the scene, and we all revered him. He was a little more out there than everybody else, and everybody was just in awe of that. When he died, the joint split apart. It wasn't the same afterwards.

BI: What sorts of things did you learn from them?

FG: For Kenny Price, Ed Moses, Ron Davis, and some of the others, the craft and the art were one. It wasn't two separate acts, and that intrigued me. I was hoping an architect could do that.

Robert Graham, *Mirror II*, 1971–73. Cast bronze, mirror. 11 x 29 x 23 inches.

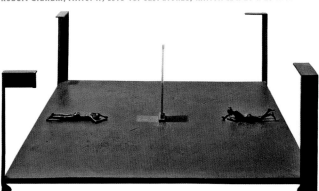

Their work was more direct and in such contrast to what I was doing in architecture, which was so rigid. You have to deal with safety issues—fireproofing, sprinklers, handrails for stairways, things like that. You go through training that teaches you to do things in a very careful way, following codes and budgets. But those constraints didn't speak to aesthetics. When I got close to these guys, I'd hang out at their studios and watch them work and observe how they dealt with things, and it was very different. I was terribly enamored with the directness of it and the Mount Everest–ness of it, how they had to confront a white canvas. That whole process seemed so much more likely to produce beautiful work than the architectural process did. I knew pragmatic things had to be taken care of, and I could do that, but it wasn't enough.

The way these artists thought and approached making things was a lot more intuitive and in touch with who they were. It seemed that was the way to find your voice, not the way I had been doing it. So I started mimicking their process, which was hard to do in architecture. And of course now you can see where it led.

BI: Let's talk about specific influences. Perhaps the painter Billy Al Bengston?

FG: Billy Al was amazing. He still is. He could fix trucks and cars and motorcycles and he could paint like a motherfucker. If you're ever caught on a desert island, you'd want Billy there with you because he would figure out how to turn coconut milk into alcohol. He knocks out walls, does plumbing, changes lights, designs light fixtures, builds lofts. I would visit him on Monday, and on Friday, his place would be all different. Architecture took so much longer.

BI: Several of those artists were experimenting with architecture then. How did that influence you?

FG: Ed Moses was designing a studio on the beach in Venice, and since I was working then on the Danziger studio, we started talking. We talked about materials, and he brought me corrugated metal and started talking about it. But then he copped out and he made it in stucco, like the Danziger studio, and I was very disappointed because I thought his corrugated metal idea was better. It was more lively and more exciting. It was newer.

BI: And Larry Bell. Wasn't he also influential during this period?

FG: Larry Bell had a very narrow space on Market Street in Venice where he built a little stairway up to his loft. The idea for the stairway came out of a horror movie with Boris Karloff, and it was familiar to me from the movie, but it was made in cheap wood. And in the dining room, there weren't just pictures on the walls. There was a hole in the wall where you saw the studs inside, with glass on either side. So you were looking at the wood studs as if they were a picture, and I loved that.

Billy Al Bengston, *I Married a Woman*, 1970. Lacquer and polyester resin on aluminum. 20 x 20 inches.

I then went on to use the corrugated metal. I thought maybe I would have gotten there by myself, but Ed sort of energized it. And I was on to the exposed studs, because of my training in Japanese wood architecture. So it was pre-ordained almost that I would go there. The rawness of everything didn't come from Ed Moses or Larry Bell.

BI: So where did it come from?

FG: I was very interested in the direct link between intuition and product. If you look at a Rembrandt painting, it feels like he just painted it, and I was looking for that immediacy in architecture. There were tract houses being built all over the place, and everybody, including me, said they looked better raw. So I started playing with that aesthetic.

BI: What else was going on around that time?

Robert Rauschenberg, *Factum 1*, 1957. Combine, 61½ x 35¾ inches, The Museum of Contemporary Art, Los Angeles, The Panza Collection, Art © Rauschenberg Estate/Licensed by VAGA, New York, New York.

FG: My quantum leap and confidence in doing that stuff came from none other than Robert Rauschenberg and probably, to some extent, Jasper Johns. Before I knew him, I dropped dead with excitement over those early Rauschenbergs. I'd come out of Victor Gruen's office, where I was trained by a Viennese master to seek perfection. But I didn't have the money to do that, and I was looking at these tract houses. I'm thinking, If you can't beat 'em, join 'em—take it as a virtue and see what you can do with it. Having the example of Rauschenberg and Johns, who used detritus to make art that people loved and paid lots of money for, opened the door for me.

BI: You've talked about yourself as a sponge during this period.

FG: I was taking it all in. It didn't matter where it came from. I kept my eyes open and watched what everybody was doing. I was ravenous for visual information. It wasn't about reading books or verbal intellect. I had done some of that in my younger days, at college and after college, but this took me on a different track, which I loved. So I just drank up painting and sculpture. I was in New York a lot, and there were bars where a lot of artists went, and I'd hang out with guys there like [the sculptor] John Chamberlain.

BI: How did you meet the New York artists you've worked with so much over the years, people like Richard Serra, Claes Oldenburg, and Coosje van Bruggen? Even Rauschenberg?

FG: This particular group of Los Angeles artists nurtured a kind of creativity that grew out of their lifestyle, their politics, their sense of who they were. All that attracted a lot of artists from the East, and many of them also came out

Claes Oldenburg, Frank
Gehry, and Coosje van
Bruggen at Gehry's office,
September 1988

here to make prints at Gemini [artists' workshop]. Through Gemini and Gemini's Elyse and Stanley Grinstein and Sid Felsen, I got into that scene. I met Rauschenberg, and we really hit it off. I used to go to his studio on Lafayette Street in New York, and we would stay up until four in the morning talking about things. I just really enjoyed him. That's when I met Jasper Johns and Claes Oldenburg, Roy and Dorothy Lichtenstein.

BI: The minimalist Carl Andre was a hero of yours, too, at one point, wasn't he?

FG: I'd gone to Kynaston McShine's Jewish Museum show, "Primary Structures," in 1966, and there was this row of bricks. I followed the bricks to a wall where a sign described the artwork as 137 firebricks by the artist Carl Andre. At that time I was doing the chain-link stuff, and I had this fantasy that you could call in architecture. You could call the chain-link guys and you could give them coordinates and they could build a structure. It would be instantaneous. I was always looking for a way to get to spontaneity, and when I saw these bricks, I thought, Carl Andre did it. He called the brick guys and said, "Set 137 firebricks in rows." He just explained it over the phone.

Well, I couldn't sleep that night. I had to meet this guy, Carl Andre. Then, maybe a few weeks later, I did meet him and I told him how I had just seen his piece at the museum and I was so fascinated by it because all he had to do was call it in. I went on and on about how wonderful it was that he'd done that, and then he looked at me like I was a madman, telling me, "You don't understand." He pulled out a pad of paper and started drawing firebrick, firebrick, firebrick on the paper. He said, "It's about the tactile quality of picking up the brick and putting it in place." That's when I realized it was painterly. It kind of put me in my place, and I loved it because it made me understand how much I really didn't know about art.

BI: Unlike the visual arts, architecture goes through so many hands. That has to make a difference.

FG: Building a building is like berthing the *Queen Mary* in a small slip at a marina. There are lots of wheels and turbines and thousands of people involved, and the architect is the guy at the helm who has to visualize everything going on and organize it all in his head. Architecture is anticipating, working with and understanding all of the craftsmen, what they can do and what they can't do, and making it all come together. I think of the final product as a dream image, and it's always elusive. You can have a sense of what the building should look like and you can try to capture it. But you never quite do.

BI: This seems like a great time to be pursuing those dream images in architecture. I don't remember architects and architecture being quite as recognized and acknowledged in the past.

FG: The AT&T Building did it, I think. That's when Philip Johnson got on the cover of *Time*. Philip was the great provocateur, spokesman, intellectual. He had a good sense that we have all gone through the looking glass.

BI: Meaning what?

FG: That there weren't that many things that were right or wrong in the visual world. There's a lot of freedom, in other words. If you could build it in real time and with real budgets, you could do it. You have to be aware of safety, and there are plenty of constraints—of the construction industry, safety requirements, availability of material, budgets, all those things—that would hold you into some kind of rationality, or irrationality, depending on how you're looking at it. Yet there is also a freedom, and I think Philip understood that. He was the one guy I could talk to straight like that, because the tendency of our colleagues is to create laws and rules.

BI: How did that relate to your own sense of freedom living in Los Angeles?

FG: Well, in the 1940s and 1950s, right after the war, you had stick architecture. Plaster. Wood. Stucco. Buildings went up so fast nobody paid much attention. People were interested in the front door, the little picket fence, a few trees. But the places were stucco. The only people who started thinking about that were Schindler and Neutra and the Case Study House architects [who were commissioned to design and build low-cost, innovative model homes after World War II].

In a way Ventura Boulevard [in Los Angeles's San Fernando Valley] is kind of the ultimate expression of that period. Because I was a truck driver out there, I saw it going up. I saw people building it. And on an individual basis, piece by piece, it was an abhorrent thing. I just hated it. And I thought, God, this is really terrible. But today it's iconic in its totality and it would be devastating to tear it down. You see how this agglomeration became something. There is no rule to it. It's not great architecture. I'm not claiming it is. But compared to other parts of the city it's quite magnificent.

BI: It's quite magnificent because . . .

FG: Because it's like a modern Fifth Avenue, but done in cheap materials. That's the scale of LA, as a drive-by. It's sort of the same commercial stuff, all of the same instincts, but on the cheap. For $1.95. Instead of stone, it's all plaster and cheap metal, signs, window frames and pillars. It's a mélange. It's a real mess. If you tried to analyze it, you'd say, "Okay, this is the reality you guys are talking about, you people who have taste and are skeptical about what an architect like me would do, or what an artist does. You are in total denial about what your built environment is like and which you allow to happen, then participate in and say is normal."

The best example for me is Paris. If you walk down the Champs-Élysées all those buildings midblock are façades. When you get to the end of the block and look at the corner buildings, sometimes the façade goes around the corner, but sometimes it doesn't. If you were to look at the backs of those buildings, you'd see they don't finish the backs. So there's a whole visual presence of the backs of buildings in conflict with the stone façades, and you see it all through Paris. I don't think the Parisians ever look at those things. They're in denial about that part. They're only looking at the façades, so nobody pays attention to the other part.

It's the same thing everywhere. Two-thirds of a building is the back end, the sides. That's what they're living with, and they put this little façade on. You can see it here. You can see it everywhere. You can see it in the Renaissance.

It's like the grande dame going to the ball with her Oscar de la Renta outfit, or whatever, with a hair curler in back which she forgot to take out. You wonder why they don't see it, but they don't. Then in comes a guy with something that is thought out and potentially beautiful. Maybe it's not beautiful by definition in their world, but it may over time become beautiful if you live with it, which is what happened to Bilbao and to Disney Hall. But in the first showings of them, people thought I was bonkers.

Over time, if they're any good, they become iconic and accepted and change people's minds about what's beautiful. Or they accept it as beautiful. And I think that happens because they're well thought out in terms of human scale and function. They really work.

BI: I'm remembering the strong reactions to your house in Santa Monica when you first redid it in 1978. Your framing a traditional bungalow with that industrial-style second structure of chain link, plywood, and corrugated metal didn't sit too well with your neighbors. Now the house is so revered you've told me you wish you'd sold popcorn to all the architecture students, architects, and critics who've since tramped through it. Can you give me a little history on the house?

FG: Berta and I got married in 1975, and our son Alejandro was born right away, the first year we were married. We were living in Ocean Park in an apartment building I had done, where I cut a hole through the walls so we had a one-bedroom and a two-bedroom joined, and we had a housekeeper live in to take care of Alejandro. But when Berta became pregnant with Sam, we knew the apartment wasn't going to work anymore. We needed a house.

I told Berta I didn't have time to find a house, and because we liked Santa Monica, she got a realtor there. The realtor found this pink bungalow on a corner which, at the time, was the only two-story house in the neighborhood. We could have moved in as it was. The upstairs part was large enough for our bedroom and a room for the baby. But it needed a new kitchen and the dining room was tiny—a little closet. The downstairs was a bit claustrophobic.

I started working on its design and got excited about the idea of building a new house around the old house. Nobody realizes I had done the same thing a year before in Hollywood, when the office was out of work. We figured we could both create work and make money. We had all chipped in and bought the house, then remodeled it. We built a new house around the old house, and the new house was in the same language as the old house. I liked that idea and I hadn't really explored it enough, so when I got this house, I decided to take that idea further.

BI: You've often referred to the house as your architectural laboratory. How did Berta feel about all that?

FG: Berta was a great client.

BI: As we all know, the house became legendary. One writer called it "the house that built Gehry." When you look back on it now, does it seem like a career marker to you?

FG: The media called it that. It was the most freedom I'd had at that point. I could express myself more directly, without editing. We didn't have much money then either. I was doing a house for [the businessman and art collector] Freddie Weisman down at the beach, and he loaned me the money for the down payment. I think we started out to spend forty or fifty thousand dollars and we ended up spending maybe a hundred thousand over time. That was a lot, because we had paid a hundred and sixty for it.

My house couldn't be built anywhere but California, because it is single glazed and I was experimenting with materials that are used here. It's also not

Gehry's 1978 Santa Monica
residence has been called
"the house that built Gehry."

an expensive construction technique. I was using it to learn the craft, to try and figure out how to use that. There was also something about the blurring of the edges between past and present that worked. People came in and asked if things like stains were intentional. We magically made a point where you weren't sure, which kind of gave it a strength. I think that's what people liked about it.

BI: In Sydney Pollack's documentary, *Sketches of Frank Gehry,* the architect and critic Charles Jencks recounts that you were shaving one day, didn't have enough light, and punched a hole in the ceiling. Is that true?

FG: No. I consciously went to the house. I wanted a window in the bathroom, so I took a hammer and punched a hole in the ceiling with the hammer. Then I put a piece of glass on the outside roof with heavy sealant so it would stay and so it wouldn't leak. That became the bathroom window. It was done like that.

BI: But it was done in the spirit of the house?

FG: Yes. Remember that on the first iteration of the house, I didn't have a lot of money to play with. It was an old house, built in 1904, then moved in the 1920s from Ocean Avenue to its present site in Santa Monica. I couldn't afford to fix everything, and I was trying to use the strength of the original house, so that when the house was finished, its real artistic value was that you didn't know what was intentional and what wasn't. You couldn't tell. It took all those clues away, and in my opinion that was the strength of the house. That's what made it mysterious to people and exciting.

Arthur Drexler [the longtime, influential curator and director of the Department of Architecture and Design at the Museum of Modern Art, who died in 1987] attended a dinner in my house once when I wasn't there. Then he went back to New York and was deprecating the house. He didn't like it, and he didn't like my work. He thought it was a joke. And the thing that he found the funniest was he saw a smudge on the wall and didn't know whether it was there on purpose or not. That was his sort of put-down remark.

Gehry redid his Santa Monica home a second time in 1991 to accommodate the needs of his growing children and to upgrade electrical and other systems.

BI: But he was looking at it exactly the way you wanted him to look at it, wasn't he?

FG: Yes. But he didn't know that he was looking at the essence of the design. Had he understood that, it would have clicked into place and he would have seen that it was something else.

BI: The house changed when you remodeled it the second time in 1991, didn't it?

FG: It did. The kids needed bedrooms and stuff, and we had more money to spend. We built a pool. We fixed the roof. We fixed the skylights and the electrical system. A lot was done that unraveled that old house, and I lost it. The house now has vestigial reminders of the old strength, but it's not as good a house. It's not as good a piece of art, if you want to call it art, as it was on the first go-round. That's my opinion, although I'm pretty sure it would be shared by others who knew both. But I couldn't do anything about it. I had to lose it because I needed the room for the kids, and there was no way to preserve that original idea without contriving it in a second instance, and I didn't want to do that. So I just charged ahead and took it on the chin. Took one for the team.

PART 2 · INNOVATING

Gehry innovations in form and materials include, from top to bottom, the Frederick R. Weisman Art Museum in Minneapolis, the Experience Music Project in Seattle, and the Center for the Visual Arts at the Toledo Art Museum, at the University of Toledo.

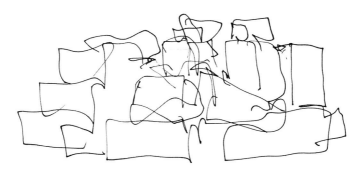

AS ARCHITECTURE STUDENTS and practitioners trekked through Gehry's residence, tour buses weren't far behind, and the architect's home began to acquire a Graceland-style patina. His confidence and reputation both on the incline, Gehry soon ventured from chain link and plywood to steel, copper, and titanium, creating buildings that were more and more sculptural.

In his home city of Los Angeles, Gehry continued moving toward larger-scale projects. In the late 1970s and early 1980s, he expanded his idea of architectural "villages" from homes to such places as Loyola Law School and Edgemar, a cultural and commercial project in Santa Monica. Another architect was selected to design the new Museum of Contemporary Art (MOCA)

Gehry designed Loyola Law School in Los Angeles over many years, starting in 1978.

in Los Angeles, but Gehry was hired to renovate a downtown warehouse as MOCA's "temporary" housing, then known as the Temporary Contemporary and today called the Geffen Contemporary at MOCA. Although Gehry reportedly called himself "a janitor" in terms of redoing the structure's barn-like interior, the *New York Times* art critic John Russell called the new museum "a prince among spaces." Today the 1983 facility is widely considered one of the first successful museum spaces of that scale to inhabit a renovated building or warehouse.

In the mid-eighties came both a major retrospective of his work, an exhibition at the Walker Art Center in Minneapolis that traveled to New York, Los Angeles, and elsewhere, and his Japanese debut with the Fishdance Restaurant in Kobe. A few years later, he competed for and eventually won the coveted commission of designing the Walt Disney Concert Hall, an undertaking that began in 1988 and stopped and started until the building finally opened in 2003.

During that period, he designed domestically such groundbreaking structures as the University of Toledo's Center for the Visual Arts at the Toledo Museum of Art, the University of Minnesota's Frederick R. Weisman Art Museum in Minneapolis, and the Experience Music Project in Seattle.

The Guggenheim Bilbao opening in 1997 capped many years of European success for Gehry as well, including such innovative projects as his Vitra Design Museum in Weil am Rhein, Germany, which he began in 1987, and in Prague, the Nationale-Nederlanden Building, better known as "Fred and Ginger," which was begun in 1992. Buildings in Germany and elsewhere followed over the years, and several more are today either in design or under construction across Europe.

When Gehry's new American Center opened in Paris, the New York Times *architecture critic Herbert Muschamp called it "witty, urbane, and as affable as Gene Kelly." For Muschamp, the American Center showed "that American architects can do more than exploit the Old World. They can enrich it."*

BI: You've often mentioned your work and friendship with Rolf Fehlbaum, the owner of Vitra International furniture company, who became, in the 1980s, your first major patron in Europe. How did the two of you meet and start working together?

FG: Many years ago, I got a letter in the mail from Rolf, who I did not know, asking me to design a chair. I put his letter in my hold box—the same hold box that's still in my office—and as happens with so many things that go in that hold box, I never looked at it again.

BI: Given that you had already designed other furniture by that time, weren't you even tempted?

FG: Well, any normal person would have thought this is a chance to do something in Europe and would have called the guy. I had designed my Easy Edges chairs already, and it was a chance to do furniture for a European furniture maker. But I put the letter in the file because I thought the only way I can do a piece of furniture is to do it like I did Easy Edges, where I set up a shop, get some people, and explore the idea. I'd be able to develop it and work on it while I was doing my other stuff. That's an expensive way to do it, though, and I felt this guy would never be interested in funding such a thing.

A sketch, a model, and a photograph of Der Neue Zollhof, a commercial complex in Düsseldorf

Maybe six or eight months later, I get another letter. I look at it and think, Well, the guy is really interested. Maybe he would be willing to finance it. Then I tell myself, You know, these furniture guys don't do that. So I put that letter in the hold box, too.

Then one day when I was in New York, I get a call from Claes Oldenburg and Coosje van Bruggen inviting me to dinner with Rolf.

BI: What did they tell you about him?

FG: They said he'd commissioned them to do a piece for Vitra in Basel, and that he'd like to meet me. I remember they also said, "He's been writing to you and you never answer." So I went to dinner, and I met him. He was an extremely nice guy. Very easy to talk to. Very friendly. He said that he really wanted me to do a chair, and I told him that I didn't think I could because of the way I work. I would need to set up a laboratory to do it, and it was probably not possible for him to do that. He agreed with me that it was impossible, so we had a nice dinner and decided that some day over the rainbow we would do a chair together. And that was that.

I then went to Europe with the Oldenburgs and my kids. We were doing a studio project with a school in Milan, and after that we went to Basel, because the Oldenburgs were placing their piece *Balancing Tools* on the Vitra site. Since I was there, I gave them some ideas. They were very happy with what I suggested, and I connected again with Rolf. We had dinner, and we all liked each other. A while later, Rolf called me to do a building. That was a surprise to me, because I wouldn't try and get a building. I never try to get a building. It happens or it doesn't happen.

BI: What did he want?

FG: It was a little furniture museum that he wanted to do as a gift for his mother. The Oldenburgs' *Balancing Tools* was a gift for his father. But the museum was so tiny, I told him it was too small for me to do. I said that the fees and flying me over there would bog him down. He told me that he was doing a factory with it, but that he didn't think I would want to do a factory. I disagreed, so I asked, "Why don't you let me do both, so it's a bigger project?" And that's what we did.

Sketch for Vitra International headquarters in Birsfelden, Switzerland (top), with model and photograph of the Vitra Design Museum, Weil am Rhein, Germany. Gehry's work at Vitra launched a friendship with Rolf Fehlbaum, his first major patron in Europe.

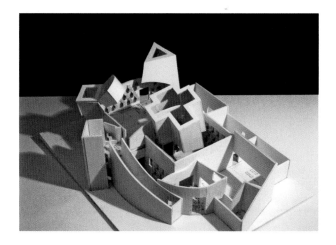

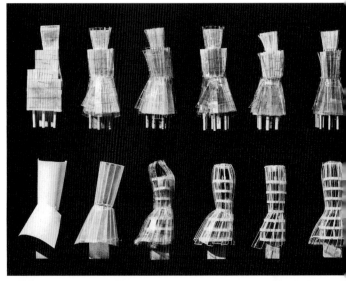

Nationale-Nederlanden Building, Prague,
Czech Republic, 1996, sketch and models

BI: Vitra seems to be an early example of the swooping, sculptural designs that you have used in so many buildings since then.

FG: Well, I never did get to finish the trellis for Norton Simon's beach house, where I was experimenting with movement. The first time I got to realize that idea of movement was in Vitra.

Vitra was followed several years later by Gehry's Nationale-Nederlanden Building in Prague.

Fred Astaire and Ginger Rogers dance in a scene from the 1936 movie *Follow the Fleet.*

BI: Much has been made of the unusual forms of your Nationale-Nederlanden Building, affectionately known as "Fred and Ginger." Is it true or apocryphal that you created the waist for your Ginger tower to permit better views for people in existing buildings who would otherwise not get them?

FG: When we began, I was thinking about the language of the nineteenth century and the neighboring buildings and of their relationship to the river.

Gehry uses a photograph of Prague's historic district to indicate what came next.

FG: Look at this balcony of an existing building with a view of the castle across the river, which my tower would block. So I pinched in my building. We were partners with the [Czech-based] architect Vlado Milunic, who thought it now looked like a female figure which Vlado called Ginger. So I called the other one Fred, and we had Fred and Ginger.

Now that was just between me and Vlado, except that he referred to them that way to the press, and once he did, it spread like fire. The press started attacking me for bringing Hollywood kitsch to Prague.

BI: So there was major controversy about the design?

FG: Yes. So much so that [president of the Czech Republic] Václav Havel got involved in the discussion. When the design was shown, Havel called me in and gave me a talk on Czech cubism and abstraction. He said that the Czech culture was very visually sophisticated. They felt representation was looking backwards, so why was I introducing a representational model to the mix, when this was the twentieth century?

BI: And you said?

FG: I showed him pictures of what we were planning and told him I was very aware of that. He was also a friend of Vlado's, and he trusted Vlado. So he was reassured, and we had a good meeting.

BI: The Nationale-Nederlanden Building, which I hear is best known in Prague as "the dancing house building," was built on speculation, as was the Neue Zollhof project, your three harbor-front office buildings in Düsseldorf. Do you think commercial developers in Europe are more forward-minded and sophisticated than they are in the United States?

FG: They are. Architecture is a more important topic in Europe. There's more of it, and historically, Europeans place a higher value on it. But America has been more experimental and open to change, because the context is not as overpowering as the European context. The nineteenth-century cities made it harder to experiment.

BI: Which leads us to your DZ Bank building in Berlin.

FG: That was a competition.

BI: But one factor in that competition, as I understand it, is that the exterior of the building had to keep in the style of the Brandenburg Gate on Pariser Platz.

FG: It did. The idea was to build a conference center inside. We had our model, with a courtyard, and we had a blob in the middle of the model representing the conference center. We were then going to design the conference center, but to design something like that takes a long time. We didn't have time because it was a competition, and we had a deadline. So I said to my colleagues, "You know the horse's head in the Peter Lewis house? I love that shape, and Peter isn't going to build the house. Why don't we put that in the model, temporarily, for the competition, and then if we win, we'll start over again?"

Of course, we never did. We won, and one of the reasons we won was because of the horse's head.

BI: I've heard there are lines outside the building in Berlin, just to look at that interior. And if we could just detour a minute back to the United States, your mention of the horse's head leads us to insurance magnate Peter Lewis, a formidable patron of yours. That relationship goes back many years, to the 1980s.

FG: I gave a talk in Cleveland one night, a long time ago. Peter Lewis was in the audience, but I didn't know him. Then I got a call from him saying that he bought a house and would I be interested. So I flew to Cleveland and he showed me this piece of land with an old house he wanted to remodel. I took him seriously and we started to work on remodeling it.

Then, and I forget all the reasons, he decided to tear the house down and design a new one. Meanwhile, he's now a bachelor and starting to make a lot of money in the insurance business. We design a house on the eighteenth hole of this golf course in Cleveland, so that when people are on the eighteenth hole, they're looking up at the house. At that point, I was doing the fish stuff, and we make a glass fish pavilion looking down at the golf course, like a sculpture. It would have been really cool had he done it. Since it was a glass pavilion, it could have been for parties and stuff. I also designed a very formal house, with a courtyard, in my style at that time. He loved it. But he decided one day that he wasn't going to build it.

BI: But all those years that you were working on a house for him that never was built were also years that gave you the chance to experiment. You've

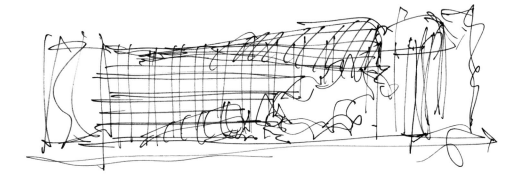

A sketch of DZ Bank, Berlin

This model and photo of DZ Bank, Berlin, emphasize the horse's head similar to the one
in the unbuilt Peter Lewis house in Ohio.

referred to it as your own MacArthur Foundation "genius" grant, and I know so many ideas from that house have wound up in your other projects.

FG: I never thought he really meant to build the house, so I was not disappointed when he didn't build it. I didn't ever count on it. I really don't know why he did it. Why he kept going with it. Why he spent so much time and money on it. I didn't ask him to. Quite the contrary, I asked him to stop. But I liked him personally, and I still do. And it turned out he did two buildings with us: the Peter B. Lewis Building for the Weatherhead School of Management at Case Western Reserve University and the Peter B. Lewis Science Library, which is under construction at Princeton.

Gehry has referred to his multiyear work on the unbuilt Peter Lewis house as his own MacArthur "genius" grant. Notice the horse's head.

BI: And what did you get out of it?

FG: What I got was an opportunity to experiment with materials, ideas, and forms. He kept asking for more collaboration, and I would bring artists around. I worked with Richard Serra on the driveway, and Frank Stella did a gatehouse. Peter, I don't think, ever intended to build any of it. But he did support it financially, for whatever it's worth. I think he spent five million in fees maybe, over a long period of time working on the house.

BI: So the MacArthur grant notion applies.

As the Peter B. Lewis Science Library at Princeton University neared completion, Gehry says, "My roots to [Finnish architect] Alvar Aalto were visible to me."

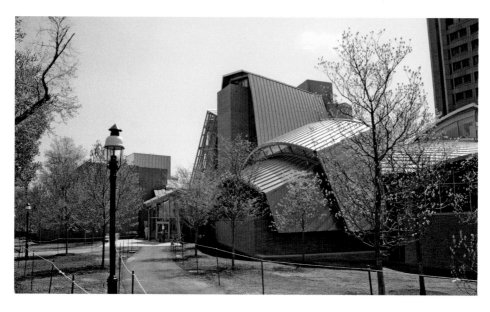

FG: I didn't treat it like that as it was happening. I was seriously trying to do stuff. You know, I've spent two million dollars on my own house, to date, over the last five years, designing it. It's been the same kind of exploration. It's just self-financed.

ART MONASTERY ON THE MISSISSIPPI

Until the Guggenheim Bilbao, Gehry's most photographed design was probably the Frederick R. Weisman Art Museum at the University of Minnesota in Minneapolis. Gehry's first U.S. museum built from the ground up, it opened in 1993. The main approach is over the Washington Avenue Bridge, and the view from the bridge is decidedly spectacular. The museum's stainless steel curves sparkle in the sun and reflect even blades of grass. An addition was also designed by Gehry.

The museum is situated on the bank of the Mississippi River, and, says museum director Lyndel King, "At our building committee meetings with Frank, we told him we wanted the museum to relate as much to the Mississippi River as to the campus. We talked a lot about the Mississippi, metal and light, and I think our building reflects that. We don't light it at night and because it's metal, it reflects the light around it. We think of it as a lighthouse, a beacon on the Mississippi.

"Frank chose a gauge of stainless steel that's thin enough so it ripples and breaks up the light in the same way the ripples on the river do. People have questioned me and probably him as well about the panels, asking if he intended them not to be smooth. The answer is yes, because it's another way the building relates to the Mississippi River, particularly when the sunset is reflected off the building in the same way it is reflected off the Mississippi. Because his buildings don't look like all the other buildings around them, people talk about Frank Gehry as not paying attention to the context of his buildings. But that's a bum rap. He pays a lot of attention to context. Our museum does not look like all the other buildings here, but it is absolutely in context with its site. Context means something more to Frank than that. It's more subtle."

BI: When I first talked with you about Disney Hall twenty years ago, you had a model of the Weisman in your office. How did it come about? Had you been to Minneapolis before?

Weisman Art Museum
director Lyndel King
refers to the Gehry-
designed museum
as "a beacon on the
Mississippi."

FG: Many times. When I was a kid at Victor Gruen's, I worked on South-dale Shopping Center in Minneapolis and I knew the Dayton family. The Dayton family collected the LA artists—my team: Ed Moses, Bob Irwin, Kenny Price, Ed Ruscha—so I used to go back with the guys for shows and openings. I met the Friedmans, Martin Friedman [the Walker Art Center's former director], and his wife, Mickey—Mildred—Friedman, who was the design curator.

BI: I know it's difficult to explain where creativity and inspiration come from, but do you have a sense of what prompted all those curved shapes on the Weisman?

FG: I don't even remember. What had we done before then?

BI: It would have been around 1990.

FG: I think we'd just worked on the American Center in Paris, where we started to introduce that kind of curve. Also, if you look at my drawings, you can see that I was thinking about Tibetan monasteries and how they looked on the hillside. When you approached the site from the Minneapolis side by bridge, it reminded me of the monasteries. It was very high from the floor level of the building down to the riverbed, maybe a couple hundred feet, maybe more. I had a façade facing the river, and that's what I started drawing.

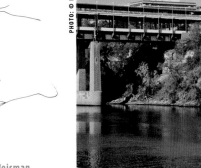

PHOTO: © DON F. WONG

Gehry says the site for the Weisman reminded him of Tibetan monasteries on a hillside.

BI: Let's talk about the drawing for a moment, not just on the Weisman, but generally. Do you just sit in a room and think? Do you walk on the beach? How does it start?

FG: I do all of those things. I go sailing. When I start working, I have absorbed a lot from my meetings. I've made models, so there's both visual and verbal information in my head when I start sketching. I sketch privately— I rarely sketch with people watching me—and I usually do it at home or on airplanes or whenever I'm alone for extended periods. Then I bring the sketches into the office. My colleagues can read my sketches, and they start making models based on the sketches. And those early models are very squir- relly; they can look like squiggly paper and trash.

We make a lot of models and we study them. Then we analyze the surface areas from a cost and engineering standpoint. It takes a long time.

BI: What are you trying to do when you sketch?

FG: I'm trying to find the answers. If you look at Michelangelo's [sixteenth- century sculptural series] *Slaves,* you realize how he carved into the stone searching for the answer, and when I draw, it's a lot like that. I'm looking for the idea. It's hand-to-eye coordination, but it's also intuition. It has the training

Squiggly paper and wood grace model for Ray and Maria Stata Center at MIT

of the language that you've evolved. I purge the obvious stuff out during those drawings, then discard *my* obvious responses and go beyond.

BI: So by the time you're sketching, you have a real sense of the project?

FG: Yes. By the time I start sketching, I understand the problem, its scale, context, budget, and constraints. So the drawings are very well-informed. They're not just fluff. I think that's why, when you see them at the end, when the project's finished, they have a lot to do with the finished building. It's because they were drawn with that information in hand. And I learn all the constraints that I'm going to have to consider by making the block models of the site.

BI: These are after the sketch?

FG: No. Before the sketch.

BI: Would all the discussions with the client come before the sketch?

FG: Well, sometimes if I look at the site and meet the people, I'll start sketching. But they're not very well-informed sketches. The sketches that are more

Gehry compares how he searches for ideas through his drawings to how Michelangelo carved into stone searching for answers.

meaningful are the ones that are done after I've made the block models, understand the terrain and the problem, and I've talked to the client.

BI: Let's go back further, then, to that talk with the client.

FG: Usually a client comes in with a program and the program has so many square feet for this and so many square feet for that. They tell me what they're trying to achieve. We make site models, with the surrounding environment, in two or three scales sometimes. It depends on the project. Then we put in blocks that represent the area and volumes of the program. When you put those on the site model, you get a clear picture of the mass you're going to be creating in relation to neighboring buildings. It gives you a picture before you design. Then I analyze the program in my sketches. I go through those different iterations, those different possibilities.

BI: How long does it usually take you to do a sketch?

Gehry looks at his watch, draws an image of a building on a notebook, then looks at his watch again.

FG: Fifteen seconds. But I do a lot of them. I circle the field for a while until I find one I like. The design team has block models, and they start adding what they see in the sketches and it gives us a place to start. It doesn't look like anything I had in mind, but at least it's something to dislike and so you start working against it.

BI: So you'll make several sketches?

FG: Yes. Then I'll move the blocks around. We do a lot of different things, and I'll have meetings with the people here and talk about it.

BI: How did this process manifest itself at the Weisman?

FG: [Gehry design partner] Edwin Chan literally took my sketches and started making models out of them. A lot of it came out of my sketches, which are very free and expressive, yet pretty well-informed in terms of scale. I'm sketching with information. I start to free-associate on this slippery paper with my pen, and it's kind of like a dance. It's free association.

BI: Informed free association.

FG: Yes. It's not just arbitrary. It comes out of a brain informed about the program, the scale, the size. It's hard to say all these important things are in it, but they are. Something's informing this hand to move like that. It doesn't just happen. There's a relevance to the images, and I start building on that.

Now here's something I'd like to say. In the case of the Weisman, if you go back to the earlier sketches, because I was insecure about it, I let the models inform the design and distort the shapes into something else. Had I stuck with the original shapes, I think it might have been better. I let that go because of insecurities, I guess.

Now I don't edit like that so much. I try and maintain the movement and character of the sketches. Bilbao was more about that. Bilbao is much closer to the sketches. It took a while for me to trust myself. It's hard, because you look at it and you say, "Oh, well, that happened too easily. You've got to suffer a little more."

When a client hires you and you do that first sketch, the client looks at it and says, "That—yes." Then they can't figure out why it takes you so long and why it costs so much to get from there to the finale. They say, "Well, you did the sketch. That's great. Just build it." That's what [businessman and philanthropist] Eli Broad didn't get when I was designing his house several years ago. Eli had problems with that idea. It confused him, because he said, "Well, I liked the first scheme, I liked the second scheme, and I liked the third scheme. Why did you keep changing it?" I wasn't changing it. It was the same idea evolving, but he saw it as wasting money.

BI: That must happen a fair amount to you, doesn't it?

FG: The drawings and first sketches are always exciting to me and exciting to clients, and I explain to them that the building goes through an evolution to achieve what the sketch is. It evolves from that, and it usually gets better. The building has to be designed from the inside out, and whatever the program is, it has to work, and you can't know all of that in the first sketch. Client programs evolve as clients see the options, explore them and make decisions. Then, the same way, the architecture responds to the client's changing decisions. So it's an evolution.

Eli didn't understand all the agony I had to go through to get that first sketch into a finished building. Now he's having fun watching me do it on my Venice house—*he's* not paying for it. In the end, my house is going to be a lot better and he'll realize it, but by the time it happens it will be five years from now and I'll be dead and he'll be dead, so we won't care.

BI: But meanwhile . . .

FG: He's laughing at me, because in his mind, this proves he was right: I just can't make up my mind, and therefore I waste a lot of time. The very first sketch was great, so why don't you just build it? There's some truth in that, but it cuts both ways. You can't really make a formula. The reason my own house in Venice has not gone forward is there are so many psychological factors beyond just drawing a sketch. To get that all right is a lot more trouble.

Digression over, Gehry returns to the subject of the Weisman.

FG: We started talking about the Weisman. I always spend a long time looking at the site and thinking about what's contextual. The site was on the side of the Mississippi, and it faced due west, so it had a western orientation. And I was thinking about the University of Minnesota buildings that have been built. About the president of the university telling me that he didn't want another brick building.

Models for the Frederick R. Weisman Art Museum in Minneapolis

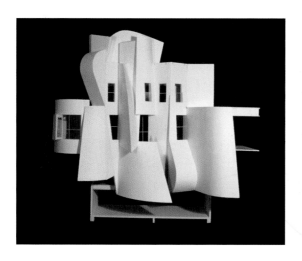

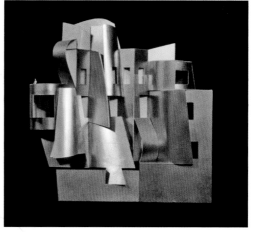

BI: Which led to the metal cladding?

FG: I had worked with metal already, so I was into it. Then Edwin and I started playing with the surface and curving it like sails, like I always like to do. Then we made it in metal, and we had this nice sculptural façade. But I was agonizing over which metal, and I had mock-ups made of the metal that we eventually used and of a duller metal.

Then I went to Minneapolis with my son Sam, who I was taking to hockey camp in Minnesota. We stopped by and looked at the site on our way up, and a week later, when I picked him up, we looked at it again. I was tending toward the duller metal because I was a little worried that the other would be very pushy. So the first week we looked at it, I convinced myself that we should use the duller surface. But when I came back the week after with Sam, he said, "Pop, go for it, it's going to be great." And he was only what—twelve years old? Somehow that gave me the courage to do it.

When the sun hits it, it reflects everything. It asserts its presence in the middle of all this brick stuff, and it called attention to itself from the Minneapolis side, which is what they wanted.

BI: How do you analyze the way the light plays off that metal? Do you sit in a room experimenting with how the light hits the model?

FG: Well, this one was easy. I realized that would happen. You see reflections on buildings.

BI: I was told that you left models outside for an entire year to see how different seasons would affect the building. Had you ever done that before?

FG: I don't know if I'd done it before, but we've done it since. In Bilbao, we did it. We did twenty-five sheet metal mock-ups, maybe more, and spent time looking at them in different light. I didn't see them every day, of course, but I went there fairly regularly to look at them. They were up for a year, I think.

BI: Were there problems with construction of the Weisman's sculptural forms? This was certainly a different sort of building for the workers, who, according to the museum's website, even had assorted nicknames for some of the design elements. Were they also skeptical about everything working out?

FG: No, we work pretty well within the existing construction industry framework. There were problems in the past, on Disney Hall for instance, where the steel framing was unusual. Because something looks slightly different from what they've bid on and accepted, they say they didn't realize it was that complicated. Our using the computer makes a difference, because the computer shows—in 3-D, not just in 2-D—all of the connections and things so they can't come back and say they didn't understand.

BI: Now you're adding on to the Weisman's existing building. Did you think of it as complete at the time, or did you always know you'd come back and finish it?

FG: We had designed more wings, but they didn't have the money for it. Although we didn't finish the design, we planned for the additions.

BI: The Weisman is the rare example where you are expanding a museum you yourself designed. There have been so many museums and other projects

A model for the Weisman expansion

Gehry is overseeing underground expansion and building renovation for the Philadelphia Museum of Art.

over the years where you've had to come in and respond to the work of other architects who got there first. I think of the Norton Simon Museum of Art in Pasadena and your work there. You've been complimented for your "respectfulness" on that remodel, and I've read that at the Philadelphia Museum of Art, where you are designing an underground expansion, officials visited the Simon Museum to get a sense of your work. How did the Simon job come about?

FG: I was on the museum board and did it for free. [Norton Simon's widow, the actress] Jennifer Jones Simon hooked me into it. Two years after Norton died, she said, "The museum doesn't look good. Something's wrong. I don't know what it is. Would you come out and look at it?" I did, and I realized what was wrong: the paintings were hung chronologically with no hierarchy as to which ones were better. But I wasn't an expert on nineteenth-century French painting, so I asked Jennifer if I could enlist help. I brought in John Walsh, who was then director of the Getty Museum and is an expert on Dutch and French painting of the nineteenth century, and I brought in [Rembrandt scholar and former director of Harvard's Fogg Art Museum] Seymour Slive. I asked Carter Brown, former head of the National Gallery of Art in Washington, who was a friend, and Irving Lavin, the distinguished scholar from Princeton. Plus several others. These were all separate flybys by these people.

I said to them, "Give me ten commandments for what we can do to make this building work better." The first thing they all said was tear the building down. I guess they were saying that because I was there, so we discounted that. But mostly their comments were critiques of how the art was hung and of the lighting.

The original architects, Thornton Ladd and John Kelsey, did those continuous curving walls that everybody is doing again now. But in the conventional sense of a museum it doesn't work, because when you get to the corner, there's no corner. Some people think you can hang a good painting anywhere, but that isn't necessarily true. So I sifted through all that and came up with a direction. Then we decided to do a modest intervention on five galleries as a test.

BI: What was your plan on this "intervention"?

FG: We started out to retain the floor and not change the walls as drastically as we did. We were not going to cut skylights.

BI: But you did all that, didn't you?

FG: Yes, but we didn't start out to do it. Then we found asbestos in the walls, so we had to seal off the five galleries. We brought in asbestos abatement people, who also found asbestos in the ceiling, and they had to take the walls out to remove it. Then it rained and water came through the skylight and buckled the wood floor. When I got there to look at it, before they were going to put it all back, it was all concrete and steel and like starting over again.

I called Jennifer and said, "You know, we're stripping this place down to zero. It doesn't make sense to put it back the way it was. It's going to cost the same to put it back in a way that you're going to like and that's going to work." She agreed, so where those curving walls were, we laid out rectilinear galleries. And in the end, we wound up with more hanging space than we had before.

BI: How does the space affect the art in museum galleries?

FG: In the beginning there's a space. Then you decide what to put in it. The space should have a persona when you walk into it. It doesn't have to, but it would be better if it does. There's an emotional something that happens,

In the late 1990s, Gehry renovated interior galleries at the Norton Simon Museum in Pasadena, California.

whether you like it or hate it. Then you can hang the art, which brings in a whole set of criteria, but it is always the space as midwife to the art and viewer. It becomes the connector between the art and the viewer.

The space can either enhance the experience or run counter to it. The assumption is you're going to hang the art in a way that people can see it at the proper height and so on, and that you're going to light it properly. In any case, whether it's in the bathroom, the dining room, or the Shrine Auditorium, whoever hangs the art is going to put it in a place so you can see it, and they'll light it so you can see it. My premise is that as long as you're making beautiful spaces, and as long as you address the technical issues, they can coexist and complement each other. The space can be an added enhancement to the experience. The most important thing is to break down the barrier between the person looking and what that person is looking at.

BI: So you see the space as more of an enhancement than prime mover here?

FG: It's ephemeral. It is sort of up for grabs. There are seven million possible solutions and no one is right. That's what I like about it.

BI: These are ideas you've also explored as an exhibition designer at museums. This seems like a good time to talk about some of the museum shows you've designed over the years.

FG: Well, the first museum show I ever worked on was the Los Angeles County Museum of Art [LACMA] exhibition "Art Treasures of Japan," in 1965. Greg Walsh, who had spent a year in Japan and knew a lot of the things they were bringing here, was invited to do the show. Since we were working together, we did it together, and it was very successful.

A few years later, Maurice Tuchman [then the museum's senior curator of twentieth-century art] asked me to design their Billy Al Bengston exhibition. At the same time, Ken Donohue, who was then the museum's director, was really suspicious of me because I was a bad boy with chain link and plywood.

BI: But the show had a considerable amount of plywood in its design.

Gehry appears amused at the memory.

FG: They didn't have a lot of money to spend on the exhibition, so I asked them what materials they had around. They took me through a shop and guess what they showed me—a bunch of dirty old plywood! So I made the whole show out of dirty old plywood, which totally fit Billy Al. Then Donohue walked through the show, and he made me paint the plywood.

BI: It was definitely an unusual-looking exhibition, especially with all the furniture. Did the furniture come from Bengston's studio or did it just look like it had?

FG: I decided to make the rooms like the artists' rooms at their studios, with their old couches. I tried to get Billy Al, his friends, everybody, to donate some of their furniture and other possessions for the show and nobody wanted to give up their couches for three months. Maybe one person loaned me some chairs.

We were at the eleventh hour and we couldn't fill the rooms. The museum couldn't afford to have me make any furniture. So I had the bright idea to go to a furniture rental place, and I rented four living rooms of furniture, sight unseen. I said, "One of each kind," and I had them delivered to the museum. We set them up as living room pieces with Billy's paintings, which were on the wall already.

Then I got a call from Maurice Tuchman, who was freaked. He said, "You better get over here. I don't think we can do this." What he realized, and what I realized, when I got over there, is that by accident we had made a colossal art piece out of those plywood walls, rental furniture, and Billy's paintings.

BI: Did you leave it that way?

FG: No, you couldn't. It preempted the paintings. It was an accident—nobody contrived it—although if I re-created that room right now, I'd be on the cover of *Artforum*. But you couldn't preempt his show. In fact, when Billy came by and saw it, he said, "Tear the whole thing down." I knew it was wrong, and I was taking it out, but he caught it before it was taken out. Then, after I took it out, he went around with his own truck and picked up artists' stuff for the show.

Several years later [in 1980], we did the Russian Constructivist show ["The Avant-Garde in Russia, 1910–1930"] at LACMA with Stephanie Barron [now the museum's senior curator of modern art]. On that one, the plywood and exposed studs worked because you could hang the paintings on the studs, and it all sort of fit together without being overpowering.

BI: The Russian show also launched an important partnership between you and Barron that has resulted in many award-winning exhibitions. You always seem to stay out of the way of the art. What are you thinking about when you're designing a show?

FG: Well, you can put any work of art in a garage filled with trash and if you light it right, it'll look fine. The only thing you feel, when you're designing a show, is that you should try and create a context that helps explain the period, the character, or whatever, without going to kitsch representations of it. You

The Los Angeles County Museum of Art has frequently employed Gehry to design exhibitions, including this one of work by Billy Al Bengston.

can usually find the essence within the work of the show, and it's just searching for that and how to put it together.

You also want to create a storyline so the show flows. The hardest time I had doing that was the King Tut exhibition ["Treasures of Tutankhamen"], at LACMA [in 1978], because of the lines of people to see everything. I went to see the show in New Orleans—or somewhere else it was before it came here— and I watched the bottlenecking, and I tried to solve that. Instead of putting the descriptive panels in the glass cases with the artworks, I put them up high so people coming toward a case could read the didactic material sooner. They didn't have to wait until they got to the case and bend over to read it. That kept the flow going.

BI: For LACMA's 1997 exhibition "Exiles and Émigrés: The Flight of European Artists from Hitler," you essentially pushed everything aside but the art. There was a white fabric scrim to hide the galleries' lights and beams, a black rubber floor and chain-link walls along the center of the gallery separating the art from related reading material.

Gehry design for Los Angeles
County Museum of Art's "Exiles
and Émigrés" exhibition in 1997

FG: That show was a straightforward idea. Exiles. Period. It required a simple response. We needed to simplify the environment by cutting out the clutter. A glass enclosure didn't quite deliver the message, but floor-to-ceiling chain link has connotations of barrier and imprisonment, is very inexpensive, and can be quite beautiful. It was an easy way to reinforce the word "exiles" with an image that was not too emotionally charged. It's there if you want to see it, not there if you don't.

BI: Stephanie Barron told me that in your exhibition design you seem to know intuitively when not to push something too hard, and I sense that philosophy in your museum gallery designs as well.

FG: The only issue about all of it is that the purists might say, "Well, if the art's the art, you don't need to do anything. Just make it a very neutral white box." But what they don't realize is that a white box is not neutral in the end.

I think that the culture of museum directors and curators is an aggravation in that they just simplistically legislate that the environment has to be neutral, so that the art can coexist. Well, there's no such thing as a neutral environment. As the white candy box becomes more and more neutral, more and more

The interior of the Guggenheim Bilbao reflects Gehry's belief that museum design doesn't have to be conventional.

perfect, it becomes more toxic to the art, because it starts to create a pristine quality that most art can't live up to. Brancusi can, but there's a lot of contemporary art that cannot. It's doing the opposite of what those curators think. In their infinite quest for neutrality, they're creating an imposition of a large magnitude. What happens over time is people get used to the white candy box, and then it becomes like white noise. You ignore it, so the container becomes more than neutral. It becomes negligible, and when it becomes negligible, it detracts from the experience of enjoying the work that they've come to enjoy.

But that's what's exciting, because you can get fifty people and each one will disagree. Which brings you back to why you do what you do. It's just an individual expression.

FINALLY, A HERO AT HOME

*G*ehry has been attending concerts since he was a boy, has long been enamored *of music, and at one point even considered learning the cello. In Los Angeles, his work in the 1970s on the historic Hollywood Bowl launched a lifelong relationship with Ernest Fleischmann, executive director of the Los Angeles Philharmonic from 1969 to 1998. Gehry's work at the Bowl spanned the years 1970 to 1982, but his Walt Disney Concert Hall saga was even longer.*

Lillian Disney, widow of Walt Disney, gave the Los Angeles Music Center $50 million in 1987 toward construction of the new hall, and following a high-profile international competition, Gehry was selected in December 1988. But a series of delays postponed completion of the hall, which finally opened in October 2003.

Before the hall was built, Gehry had often felt unappreciated in his hometown. Because he had been passed over in the competition to build the city's new Museum of Contemporary Art (MOCA), a commission which went to the Japanese architect Arata Isozaki, even the success that followed his doing MOCA's Temporary Contemporary was in many ways bittersweet for him. So when he was first approached to compete for the Disney project, he was very skeptical.

BI: Many people, even in Los Angeles, forget the years you spent working with the Los Angeles Philharmonic on the Hollywood Bowl.

FG: When Ernest Fleischmann first moved to LA, he invited me to dinner to talk about "fixing" the Hollywood Bowl. It was the kind of project I was hoping I would get someday, and I was really excited about it. So at the end of the dinner, I said I would put together a fee proposal. Then he said I didn't understand. There was no money. This was just a great opportunity for me.

I said, "Mr. Fleischmann, I can't do that. Nor would I do it. But there are architects in town who have benefited from cultural projects in the past who could probably afford to help you, like Bill Pereira, who designed the Los Angeles County Museum of Art." Ernest said, "Well, I don't want him to do it. I want you to do it." My reply was, "Well, if I do it, I would have to be paid."

I left there thinking, I wasn't going to get the job. But even at that point in my career, I would never put myself in harm's way financially. A lot of architects would probably have done it, but I didn't have any choice. I didn't have the money. It was risky to say things like that, I guess, but it wasn't "contrived" risky. I didn't say, "Well, I'm going to tell him this, and he'll come back." It wasn't like that at all. I assumed he would never come back. But he did. He called the next week and asked how much it would cost, and I negotiated a ten-thousand-dollar fee.

After many delays, the Walt Disney Concert Hall opened in 2003.

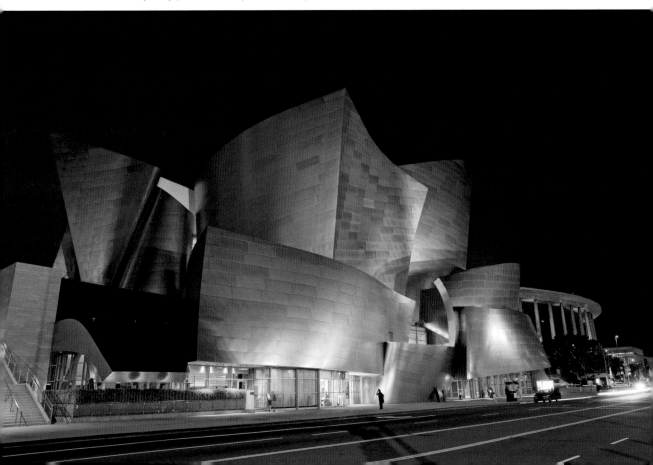

"Sonotubes," cardboard tubes, were in place at the historic Hollywood Bowl from 1970 until 1980.

BI: Was that a lot of money at the time?

FG: It wasn't much to do a thing like that, no. So then I came up with the idea of the cardboard tubes. The problem at the Bowl is that the shell focuses the sound. The musicians can't hear each other, the sound's garbled, and the tubes neutralized it. I worked with the acoustician and we sealed the tubes on the end, so there was a vibration that got a bass response. It was a temporary solution that lasted for eight years. We were going to remove the shell, which would have solved all the problems. And when that didn't get passed, we hung huge balls inside the shell, but they're gone now, too. Instead, they built a new shell to look like the old shell, which is silly as hell. But there was a lot of nostalgia for that shell, although the acoustics there never really worked.

BI: All those years working on the Bowl also clearly launched your crucial relationship with Fleischmann.

FG: It did. The Bowl began my odyssey with Ernest, which turned out to be an important odyssey. Ernest sort of taught me about music. He invited me to a lot of concerts and introduced me over the years to all the musicians. We had endless dinners with people who came to play at the Bowl and at the Music Center's Dorothy Chandler Pavilion. And we worked on the Bowl over and over again.

But when Disney Hall came up, I felt that politically I was incorrect because Buffy—[the Music Center's chief patron and fund-raiser] Dorothy Chandler—never liked my work. In her opinion, I screwed up the Hollywood Bowl.

I met Buffy Chandler when I was doing Norton Simon's beach house. Norton and his wife, Jennifer Jones, were having a birthday party for David Niven. I'm sitting there and Norton, who got wind that they were going to build a concert hall, is telling Buffy about me. So she says, "I know who Mr. Gehry is. I know what he does. I don't like his work, and he will not be considered to design a concert hall."

Just then, the woman serving the vegetables spilled the entire vegetable platter all over my new suit, which was one of those nice tan suits, not a dark one where you could simply wipe it off. There were vegetables and butter all over my suit, and one of the other dinner guests tried to be nice and change the subject by asking what other buildings I'd designed. When I said we had just completed the Ron Davis house up the street, he said, "Oh, that piece of shit!"

I got through dinner, but I remember going home thinking, Why bother?

BI: But it did lead eventually to Disney Hall.

FG: Yes, six or seven years later. It took them a while to get it together. When I first heard they were going to have a competition, I never expected to be asked. And when I got asked to be in the competition, I said no. I didn't want to be in it because I assumed it would be like MOCA, where they felt they had to have a local guy as a serious contender; I was a high-profile local guy, but I wouldn't be chosen. I said, "Guys, I've been through this so many times. Don't do this to me."

BI: You're referring to what happened with the Museum of Contemporary Art here? Let's go back to that.

FG: In the late 1970s, I had been working with [the art collector] Marcia Weisman on the Pan-Pacific Auditorium. She and her husband, Fred, were talking to the city about creating a contemporary art museum in the old Pan-Pacific, and I did studies for her on that. When it came about that the developers of California Plaza downtown could use 1.5 percent of their budget to start an art museum on Grand Avenue instead, several of us met at Marcia's house to talk about it. They told me all the artists would be getting together to discuss the museum, but I never heard from them. Then, later, I heard there was an artists' meeting, and they didn't invite me. They consciously excluded me. I asked Marcia why and she said the meeting was just for artists. But some of the artists who were there told me later that people at that meeting talked about me and decided they didn't want me involved. It was all reported to me, so I could get offended and angry, I suppose.

I have what I call an "Aw shucks" personality. It was probably a kind of protective thing for me in my growing up, that I wasn't confrontational. So a lot of my trouble with artists and with other architects over the years may have come about because they saw me as some kind of sycophant, which I wasn't. I was really excited about what they were doing, and I was excited to be part of it. But what blindsided them was that I was also doing my own stuff, too, and I also had an ego and I also was personally ambitious, and when that came out they were caught off guard by it. Some of them just gave up on me as soon as they realized I was going to create my own waves.

I think the same thing happened with the architects in New York, who were kind of attracted to me as long as I was subordinate to them. As soon as I came out with work that got attention, there was kind of a backlash from them. It's the same issue. They think I'm an "Aw shucks" guy and then I turn out to be every bit as ambitious as they are.

Being shut out of that artist meeting for MOCA hurt my feelings. It was a kind of betrayal. I probably asked for it, but I didn't go try to change their opinions. I did nothing, although for a while I didn't see some of them. It took me about two years to get over it, actually. But they fell in love with Arata Isozaki, the architect who wound up building MOCA, because of the painter Sam Francis. Sam had a relationship with Arata in Japan, and wanted him to do it, and so they all went to Japan, the whole group of them, and when you do that you fall in love with the people. And Arata was doing some interesting work.

Because the city was involved, they had to have a competition, and so they interviewed six architects. I was told they needed to include an LA architect who would be credible, and was asked if I would do it. I said, "Okay, I'll do it, but I'm going to say what I believe," and that's what I did.

BI: Knowing that you weren't really a contender?

Gehry laughs a rather rueful laugh.

FG: I knew they had picked Isozaki, so I told them what I thought would be likely problems with developers and how to handle negotiations. I told them some of the problems they could have with an architect from another country who speaks a different language, and how they might handle that. I made a few other points, showed my work, and left.

Then time passed. Pontus Hulten, who was MOCA's first director, the museum's future director Richard Koshalek, and Sam Francis invited me out to dinner. They said there was a warehouse they were going to get from the city, which they wanted to turn into a temporary building—to be called the Temporary Contemporary—and they wanted me to design it. I looked at them, and I said, "You mean a consolation prize? You don't need to do that." But they said they really wanted me to do it. They said it was going to be historic—and they were right in the end about that—and I was the only one who could do it. They weren't going to take no for an answer. I said I was going to think about it, because although I thought it was a good idea, I didn't think I should be part of it. Later they had an artists' group come and talk to me, and they wanted me to do it, too.

BI: Museum spaces like the Temporary Contemporary have become considerably more common now—the Tate Modern in London, Mass MoCA in Massachusetts, Dia:Beacon in upstate New York. But the Temporary Contemporary was probably the first alternative space on that scale to emerge in a renovated industrial building, certainly in the United States.

FG: I just tried to use it the way it was and not embellish it, because I liked the space. I helped them with the first installation, which was fun to do, and I helped with the first exhibit.

BI: What about your anger at the artists?

FG: I've learned to sublimate that anger pretty much, so I don't act it out in public. I also think that there is a certain energy that you get from it, but it's not conscious. I didn't feel consciously I was going to prove anything when I decided to do it. I took it as a real project, and I think what convinced me was Koshalek, because I thought he was sincere and he really did make me feel they weren't going to give it to anybody else. It was just me or nothing.

BI: It was also Koshalek who urged you to compete for Disney Hall, wasn't it?

FG: Koshalek said, There's going to be a competition and if you win it, you'll get the job. So, after a lot of prodding, I finally agreed to do it.

In the late 1980s, about twenty-five international architects were asked to submit information on their firms, send slides, and provide references. MOCA director Koshalek chaired the Disney Hall subcommittee of museum and university executives who whittled contenders down to six, then eventually to four: Gehry, Gottfried Böhm from Cologne, Hans Hollein of Vienna, and James Stirling from London. Gehry had yet to win the Pritzker Prize, but his three distinguished competitors already had.

BI: You never expected that you'd win the Disney Hall competition, did you?

FG: My European colleagues thought I had the inside track, but it was quite the opposite. I was the long shot. In fact, at the beginning, I was invited by Ron Gother, the Disney family lawyer, to come to his office and meet with him. He told me that I should get out of the competition because it was a waste of time. They knew my work, and there was no way the family would have Walt Disney's name on a building I designed. He actually said that.

BI: Yet you persevered. You didn't pull out.

FG: That's me. That's my work, that's what I do, and it's always going to be like that. I suppose that's what toughened me up for the future. I have to be grateful to them. But I actually tried to get out. Can you imagine if I had done that?

I stayed in and worked on the competition, and it was very difficult. I submitted the work, we had interviews, and each team made a presentation.

Meanwhile, our models were all brought to an office building nearby where everyone reviewed them. Without our names.

BI: Did the pressure ease for you at some point?

FG: The day I was to make my presentation, Gottfried Böhm and his son made their presentation just before me. He came out afterwards just ecstatic that he'd connected with the jury. He told me, "Don't bother going in. I've won it. My family and I are going to this restaurant down the street, and as soon as you're finished, come over and we'll have champagne together to celebrate." It sets you up for your presentation, right? Then, as I'm going in, I meet Ron Gother coming out, and I still remember the way he looked at me and shook his head: "You really surprised me, Frank." That's all he said.

When I went in to make my presentation, the reception was warm and friendly, and I heard over the grapevine later that we did a good presentation. The next day, the final two competitors, James Stirling and Hans Hollein, made their presentations. But I was already gone, en route to prior commitments in Europe. I was staying at a hotel in Basel when I got a call asking when I'd be back and if I could come by Lillian Disney's house at 4 p.m. on Sunday. I tried to find out more, but I couldn't.

The word was that Hollein was scheduled for 2 p.m. While it turned out not to have been true, this was the gossip that my office got. But when I went there, I didn't see Hollein leaving. I walked in and met Lillian, and we talked about the hall. She had questions. But nobody gave me any sense that I had won this. Zero. That night I got another call asking if I could be at the Music Center at 9:30 the next morning. I could bring Berta with me, but even then, I wasn't sure. I'd heard Hollein would be there as well.

When we arrived at the Music Center, we were escorted to a room and told to wait there and listen for my name to be called. I still didn't know whether we'd won it or not. I even remember thinking they may have been down to Hollein and me and that it would be like a beauty contest; Hollein was in another room somewhere, and they were going to bring out the runner-up, then the winner. But by then, I also thought there was a good chance this was it, and Berta sort of knew this was it.

A sketch for the Walt Disney Concert Hall

Gehry asks Berta to join our conversation, and she reminds him of that morning. Of "the butterflies in our stomachs the entire morning." How they held hands and their hands were ice-cold. How they kept pacing up and down. Both Gehrys appear to be choking up with the emotion of that memory, and when Gehry speaks again, he worries aloud that he might actually cry talking about it. Which he does.

FG: We stood there, in this very formal room, holding hands. Then the door was opened. I could hear a press conference starting, and a review of the competition process went on and on and on. Finally, they said they'd chosen their winner, and sure enough I heard my name called. Berta and I walked out to thundering applause. It was thrilling.

Did you see my picture in the *Los Angeles Times* and the grin on my face? You can see I was just ecstatic. It was a great breakthrough in my career, to get a project like this.

And then the saga went on for fifteen years before it was built and open.

BI: Fifteen years is a long time.

Frank and Berta Gehry attend opening night of Robert Rauschenberg's "Combines" exhibition at the Museum of Contemporary Art, Los Angeles, in May 2006.

FG: It happens all the time—you compete, you get the assignment, and then you wait. They have to fund-raise and, sometimes, like Washington's Corcoran Gallery of Art expansion, it doesn't happen. With Disney Hall, it took so bloody long to realize, with so many stops and starts, that people said it wasn't going to get built. It was only after Bilbao that the powers that be in LA realized that I did know what I was doing, and that it wasn't a folly. I guess they were also embarrassed that it didn't happen here first, though I don't really know.

So, in 1998, they resurrected Disney Hall, and I went through a whole lot of angst and agony with people on the board who wanted to control how it was done. It was the same story all over again. At one point, even though it was going to get built, they were not going to build it with me; they were going to take my design and have somebody else do it.

BI: Were they seriously considering that?

FG: Yes, they were, and I had a face-off about it. I wrote a letter and said they could use my design, but that I was going to step aside. Then word of that apparently reached Diane Disney, Walt and Lilly's daughter. She didn't really know me at that point, but she told them that the remaining twenty-five or thirty million of her mother's money would only be released to them when I told her it was okay. That's what made it possible. It was a tortured story, and it's kind of a miracle that it got built. I would credit Diane because in the end it was her move that made it happen.

That happens a lot with me. They look at what I'm proposing, what I'm working on and doing, and it seems strange to everybody, so they think it's unbuildable and impractical. People still think I don't follow programs, I don't

WALT DISNEY CONCERT HALL, LOS ANGELES, 2003.
PHOTO: © GIL GARCETTI

The Disney Hall construction was delayed for a decade.

follow budgets. That comes up in the press all the time. They are presumptions people make because of the work. But having to wait so long isn't just something that happened at Disney Hall. That's life in architecture.

THE DISNEY HALL COMPETITION: LOOKING BACK

The Getty Research Institute videotaped much of the competition proceedings, including an earnest Gehry presenting his wares to public and private arts executives for the first time. In late February 1988, in the very same room where he made his pitch eighteen years earlier to redesign the Hollywood Bowl, Gehry began his remarks by saying how pleased he was "to be part of this illustrious group you're considering." He told his audience that he actually met Walt Disney in the 1950s when working on a project at the Los Angeles International Airport, noting, "I did shake his hand. That should get me in the first door, right?"

It's vintage Gehry, a man who seems alternately ill at ease and charming. In a slide show of what he calls his "personal vocabulary and ideas," he tells the judges he wants them to understand his projects "aren't from Mars." He says a drop in the real estate market led to "some of the stuff that probably scares the bejesus out of you."

He reminds them, too, that he knows their city, having been in Los Angeles since 1947 and having graduated from USC's School of Architecture. Noting he's had his own office there since 1962, he remarks that his career "is bound to this city." He minimizes his work in chain link, maximizes his experience and achievement. Later, in response to questions, he uses music-oriented verbs like "composed" and "orchestrated."

BI: How do you go about putting together a competition entry like the one you did for Disney Hall? What was important to you to include?

FG: The whole competition was a statement of principles. I was intent on stating what I would do in as clear a way as possible, so that people evaluating it would understand what kind of architect I was, how I would approach it, and what I would do. They could see what I thought was important in the organization of the building, the relation to context, and the values that would be held to in the decisions I had to make. I wanted to state all of those principles, and I think they are very explicitly stated in my submission, both verbally in the presentation and in the written material and then in the design.

I made a fetish of being very clear on this project. I wanted them to understand what I was doing and what I was going to do, because there was a lot of anxiety about me and chain link and corrugated metal and where I came from. There had just been an article in the *LA Times* on my house, and the general public reading that kind of stuff and seeing those kinds of buildings wouldn't understand that I could do a building of this stature with the necessary commitment to materials, details, processes, surfaces, and things that would be

Gehry's Walt Disney Concert Hall competition entry, 1988

appropriate. It's really hard to live all that down. My early work was done with very limited budgets, and I made the most out of it by using those materials. What was dealt me were those kinds of buildings.

Gehry is getting more and more passionate as he speaks. It is a refrain I have heard many times through the years.

FG: I have a lot of feelings about this because you always have to work against your past. It's as though people expect you to blow one note all the time, and I guess a lot of people can only blow one note. But there are people who can blow two or three notes, and I happen to be one of them.

I tend to grow with the situation, and the situation here had many things that I agreed with. One of them was that Walt Disney's name was going to be put on this hall. He represented a certain kind of creativity and propriety, and I felt that since the hall was going to have his name and it was being given by relatives who were still alive, this building should represent Mr. Disney. That would lead you to certain choices in materials, and you wouldn't make it cheap. But also you wouldn't make it pretentious.

BI: Did Lillian Disney give you a sense of this?

FG: I found out after I met with Mrs. Disney that I was right about that. I thought that before I met her, and it was confirmed after I won. I found her to be about modesty and unpretentiousness. She wanted a building that would speak to people's perceptions of Mr. Disney.

BI: What were some of the other issues under consideration then?

FG: There was the role that this building would have in the city of Los Angeles and in relation to the multiethnic population. They talked about "the body language of the building," and the desire to make it inviting and accessible. It had to be inviting and bring you in, not put you off, so people walking down the street would not feel like this was Mount Olympus and they had to go through a formal experience to get into the inner sanctum. I believed and still believe that music is for everybody, and we all would like the multiethnic population to feel warm and welcome here. Part of Mr. Disney's genius was to contact the masses rather than just be an elitist, so that fit and was something I agreed with.

There was also the issue of the importance of the building in the community, both its symbolic importance and its importance over time. It had to be a building that had permanence and one that looked like it was going to stay there for a while.

BI: You're speaking also now of the urban context?

FG: I got very interested in the urban issues, and I walked around the city. I walked around downtown. When I first came here from Toronto with my family, I used to walk around the old Bunker Hill, and I went back and walked around. I remembered what it was before and I remembered what we lost. I thought about what was missing and what was needed. I was very concerned about the Dorothy Chandler Pavilion and the relationship of what I was going to do to the Chandler, because the Chandler was important to me. I was here when they built it, and I remembered all the hoopla. And I've said many times that regardless of what I thought about the buildings architecturally, I knew there was an emotional commitment to those buildings in the

PHOTO: © TIM STREET-PORTER

The Walt Disney Concert Hall's opening celebrations took place in October 2003.

community, and that for better or for worse, one shouldn't malign those buildings. It's not just because it was the Chandler. I always try to create an optimistic interplay.

BI: Did you express all of this to the committee choosing an architect?

FG: They asked why each of us wanted to do this project, and I put down in words what it meant to me. I decided I would throw all my cards on the table, from day one, about where I was and where I'm going. I like to do that with clients. I really feel that is important, because you're dealing with clients who don't know your process, and don't understand it.

You demystify it for them, because finally you can't tell them why you picked one form or direction or another. It's very difficult. There is a mystical part of the creative process. I don't know why I intuitively do some things. But I try as best I can to explain the driving forces and the baseline issues that I'm dealing with which lead to my conclusions. And that's what I tried to state in that first letter.

BI: It seems like you have a lot of people to please. Is that the case on any job of this scale?

FG: On any public project it is. You listen as much as you can and then you make your choices. Acoustically, there are experts so somebody else will take that heat, but I'm concerned about it enough to really participate as much as I can. I'm the architect. I'm going to take the rap, whatever it is. Good, bad, or indifferent.

BI: The well-being of the musicians was another priority, wasn't it?

FG: Yes. In my initial statement, I talked about a need to make the musicians feel important. So another big piece of this was what the building did for the musicians: what it meant to them, how they felt in it, how they got to it, their point of arrival in their cars, where they parked, where their dressing rooms were. I felt, and the client felt, all of these things were important to the success of the building because very few concert halls deal with dressing rooms and such. The message you get when you go backstage at most concert halls is that you're in a dungeon. These poor bastards: they're asked to come out onstage in their tuxes and play beautiful music, then go back in their holes.

My own life experience of giving lectures in various universities has been similar—you go to a town to give your lecture, the room you're going to speak in is cold and uninhabitable, the acoustics and equipment sometimes don't work, and you're nervous about giving the talk anyway.

Ernest Fleischmann also has a great empathy with the orchestra, and it was written into the program that the musicians would get facilities that most orchestras don't get. We thought the ambience was important in order to get people in the mood for making music.

BI: And the people who listen to that music?

FG: You want people to feel good about coming, besides just having the experience of the music. You want it to be a fabulous people experience. You want it to be comfortable. You want it to be easy.

During the day, natural light is coming in. There are five light sources. There's one in each corner that you don't see. You see just shafts of light coming into the building and not the source of the light or where it's coming from. You just see it's up there. There's also one at the top of the highest balcony seats, the rearmost seats in the hall. They're designed so that as you walk up to your seats toward the rear of the auditorium, you go towards the light, which is again symbolically a beautiful idea.

BI: Was the garden a consideration at that point?

FG: There was an issue of how to make a garden. The garden is certainly compatible with music, and a garden in Los Angeles is possible, whereas a garden in Berlin or New York is not as easily achieved. Being able to go out into the garden at the intermissions would certainly be welcome, and, coincidentally, Lillian Disney, the benefactress, loved gardens.

BI: Let me ask you what I always ask you: How do you come to all these conclusions?

FG: Well, the idea of making a populist place is something I feel very strongly. I did it in the Temporary Contemporary. I try to make all my buildings accessible. Even my house has big windows that people can see in. I'm about being as open and accessible as I can.

BI: Michael Maltzan, your project designer for the competition, said you "stew and stew and talk to people." What happens when you "stew"?

FG: I immerse myself in the project and its issues. So in the case of Disney Hall, I listen to music. I go to concerts. I talk to musicians. I talk to listeners of music. I talk to anybody who'll talk to me about what a concert hall should be.

WALT DISNEY CONCERT HALL, 2004. PHOTO: © JIM McHUGH

Many Disney Hall concertgoers walk to seats "towards the light."

BI: Who are these people? People on the street? Your friends?

FG: Well, I talk to people in the office. I talk to friends. I already had a relationship with the LA Philharmonic, and I'd talked to Ernest for twenty years. I knew a lot about what Ernest felt about music.

We developed a process that brought in conductors and other musicians, people like Pierre Boulez, Simon Rattle, whoever came to town. We asked their opinions, and we talked about their feelings. Zubin Mehta dropped in and talked to me. Boulez was a major resource. Whenever he was here, I nailed him, and whenever I was in Paris, I'd see him. With all of them, it was very helpful for me to understand the nuances of their perceptions.

BI: Esa-Pekka Salonen, who was then the Philharmonic's music director designate, also spent a lot of time talking with you, didn't he? You even made

Disney Hall benefactor Lillian Disney "loved gardens," which are easy to feature in Los Angeles.

a model of the Swedish Radio Symphony Orchestra hall in Stockholm that was comparable in size to the Disney Hall model.

FG: I pushed and pulled him into the process. The length of time everything took was discouraging, but then to have the involvement of this energy from Esa-Pekka was exciting and enlightening. We made the two models for him so he could put them side by side. He told me he really used them, studying them. It gave me a comfort zone to know that he was watching the process. He understood what it was going to be like, as clearly as I could make it for him.

BI: You're also very interested in music yourself. What is it about music that attracts you?

A model of the Disney Hall interior

FG: Well, first of all, I'm a dilettante when it comes to classical music, but I certainly appreciate it. Although I'm not knowledgeable about the history of things, I love to go to concerts and listen.

BI: Describe how you listen.

FG: When I concentrate on music, I listen to its structure. I try to understand the repetitions and evolution, because it evolves spatially for me. Some music tells a story: in Tchaikovsky, the clouds are coming and the rain is coming down. But then the more abstract Mozart, Beethoven, Bach, and contemporary music, like John Adams, don't tell a story. So you listen for the structure and you try to understand it. Sometimes you hear some familiar phrases or ideas, and sometimes you can pick up where they came from. Quite often I'll go to a concert, get very tired, and sort of float off into some kind of reverie. I'm just sort of semiconscious, and I'll find myself fantasizing spaces and shapes and things.

BI: The music will stimulate images for you?

FG: Yes. It's very much like architecture. You know, architecture has been called frozen music and somebody asked me if that means that music is liquid architecture.

BI: You've said that if you could be an instrument you'd be a cello?

FG: I love the persona of the cello, the sound of it and the image of it. I've always had a fantasy about playing the cello. I almost signed up for lessons once, maybe twenty years ago, but I realized it would be ludicrous at that point in my life. I always fantasized if I could transform myself into a musical instrument I would want to be a cello. I saw too many Walt Disney movies.

BI: You go to the symphony a lot, don't you?

FG: Not as much as I'd like. I used to have season tickets, and I used to go every week. I went to music a lot before I got involved with the Philharmonic, and I go to a lot of concerts at the Philharmonic. I always have, even before Disney Hall was built.

BI: Does that include contemporary classical music?

FG: You can't be interested in modern art without realizing something had to be going on in modern music. My sister was formerly married to the composer Mort Subotnick, but I liked electronic music before Subotnick. I used to listen to Varèse and Stockhausen.

But I also love baroque and Bach and Mozart. Vivaldi. Webern. I like the late Webern, which reminds me of haiku. I'm always fascinated with the economy of words, when somebody can say everything quickly and succinctly, and I love that in music, too. I've never been trained as a musician, but I did immerse myself in all of it.

I look at the orchestra as a sculpture. Does that make sense? I look at it three-dimensionally. While I'm listening to music, I'm looking at the forms of the people and the movement of the instruments. I study the violin and the cello and the bass.

Gehry was influenced by Japanese woodcuts and the nineteenth-century carp drawings of Ando Hiroshige.

BI: During concerts?

FG: Yes, during concerts. My fish double-curve forms are very apparent in the violin and cello; you can find fish forms in the shapes of those instruments.

BI: Let's talk about those fish forms you incorporate so often in your work. When I see one, I'm often reminded of your childhood experiences of seeing carp go from plaything to food.

FG: When we lived in Toronto, there was a Jewish marketplace there called Kensington Avenue, just a few blocks away from my grandparents' house. I'd go there with my grandmother to buy groceries, and I especially liked going on days when she would buy a carp. We would walk home with the carp in waxed paper filled with water, and when we got home, she'd put it in the bathtub. My cousins, my sister, and I would play with the fish and watch it swim around, and I remember sometimes feeding it. Then it would disappear, and we'd have gefilte fish for dinner. I didn't put the two together at first, but then I finally figured it out.

BI: Do you think that's where your preoccupation with fish began?

FG: I don't think so, but I do like carp the best. I use that image, which I think comes from my fascination with Japanese woodcuts and the carp drawings of Hiroshige.

Let me back up. I was raised in architecture as a modernist, because when I got into architecture school the Beaux Arts period was over. They had only a token class in architectural history and a token class in art history at USC at the time. Modernism was the mantra, and I bought into that. That's how I was trained.

When I went to Paris in 1960, I looked at things every weekend. That's when I saw the great cathedrals—Notre Dame, Chartres, and others—and I thought, Holy shit, I've been had. There was a toughness about them that I liked. But when I got back to Los Angeles and started my practice in 1962, I was sort of still in the modernist mode.

Then Arthur Drexler, the architecture and design curator at the Museum of Modern Art, did his big show in 1975 about the Beaux Arts, and it just took off like wildfire. Charlie Moore, Robert Venturi, Michael Graves, and everybody started doing what we call postmodern. And it freaked me out. It was decorative, soft and pandering and all the things I didn't care about, and I didn't know how to deal with it. The rest of the world seemed to be excited about it, but I was left behind. The train left the station with a new conductor and I didn't know how to get on it.

BI: Which led you to fish imagery?

FG: I got interested in the fish image when everybody started doing the neoclassical, postmodern stuff. I remember thinking that Greek classicism is anthropomorphic, and I believe it was when I was giving a lecture at UCLA that I said, "Well, if you're going to go back, why don't we go back three hundred million years to fish? If you're going to go backwards, let's go way backwards."

So I started drawing fish. I drew a lot of them. I started to look at real fish. I got really interested in them as a form and in the idea of bringing movement into architecture. It was a way of exploring double curves, which are hard to do in architecture. If you were trying to study double curves, how would you do it? You could make drawings, but of what? Here was a ready-made image.

When Gehry went to Paris in 1960, he "got pretty excited" about such great cathedrals as Notre Dame.

BI: Was this a conscious decision on your part?

FG: It wasn't totally conscious. I'll find something that intrigues me and I follow it. I trust my instincts. Also, when I talk about fish, it's sort of fun, because if you talk about doing a study of double curves, it sounds terribly esoteric and heavy-duty.

Gehry sees the influence of Romanesque chapels on his 1992 fish sculpture for the Vila Olímpica in Barcelona, Spain.

BI: So you are trying to express the idea more simply, is that it?

FG: Yes. I don't like to portray it to other people as a complicated intellectual endeavor. It is for me, but I don't like to lay that on other people. It's just something I'm interested in, and talking about it in terms of fish and fish images lightens it and makes it less of a burdensome thing.

I think it's misunderstood. People think I'm poking fun or making lighthearted jokes, but

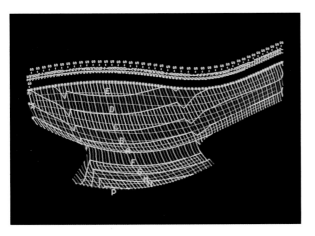

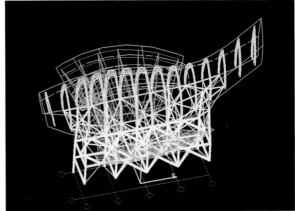

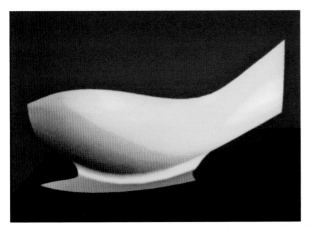

Computer and built models for Gehry's fish sculpture for the 1992 Olympic Games in Barcelona

it's certainly not that. I invest a lot of time and effort in studies, and you can see it in the work. Using double curves, I have a complete vocabulary that I can draw from, which is translated into building forms. In other words, I'm taking it from the sketch into built forms of what I'm interested in. I would bet most architects avoid double curves, like I did, because we didn't have a language for translation into a building that was viable and economical, and I think the study of fish allowed me to create a kind of personal language, which I now know how to use. So it was a demystification of that stuff, and it is an enormously important study for me.

BI: Your use of fish imagery has gone far beyond that double-curve study, though.

FG: I used a fish sculpture in the middle of a plaza I was doing in Kalamazoo, Michigan. I made the fish lamps. GFT, a high-fashion house in Italy, asked me to do a sculpture at the Pitti Palace for an exhibition in 1985, and I made a wooden fish thirty-seven feet long. People could sit in it.

This big fish also went to Turin in 1986, for the first show when they opened the Castello di Rivoli, and something extraordinary happened there. The prominent curator and museum director Rudy Fuchs was there standing beside me and I was standing beside the fish, and the fish's tail moved, in my eyes, and I thought, like Archimedes, Eureka! How did that happen? At that point, he introduces himself and he asks, "Would you have a drink with me, please?" I said sure. We went down to the bar and got a drink. Then he looks at me and asks, "How did you do that?" I said, "You noticed it?" He said, "Yes," and I realized he got the torque, the feeling as he stood beside it. Once I understood it, I then could build those kinds of shapes.

I was intrigued with movement and inert materials. I guess that intuitively I was looking for a way to express feeling in a building, without resorting to postmodernism and decoration, and how do you replace that? What do you do with the building, the space, the room, the architecture that makes it something that people respond to?

In the 1970s, I did a job for Norton Simon that also involved movement. Norton had a really beautiful Indian Shiva dancing figure on his dining room table. When I was working on his beach house in Malibu and we'd sit at the table to talk, we'd turn around and you were sure the Shiva moved. He was fascinated with that, as I was, so to please him I decided to make a trellis that looked as if you piled up a bunch of two-by-fours on the beach, then imagined a windstorm came and froze them in motion.

I told Norton I was going to do it. I did sketches and stuff, but I don't think he really believed me. But he let me rag on and actually do it. I didn't know how else to do it except to create it as we built it. So I built the first layer, the second layer, and the third layer. As I was getting ready for the fourth, he stopped me, and he said, "I've had enough of this. I'm not going any further. This will be your unfinished symphony." And I said, "But Norton, Schubert died."

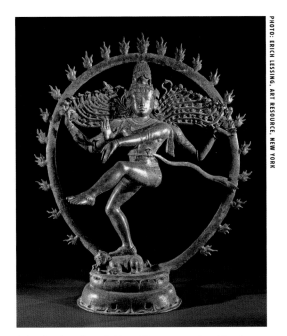

PHOTO: ERICH LESSING, ART RESOURCE, NEW YORK

Gehry has long been intrigued by movement and inert
materials, as reflected in this Indian Shiva dancing figure.

We never finished it, and I tried to incorporate the idea on the Familian
house, which never got built, and then on my own house. If a client didn't do
something, I would try it somewhere else. I would keep going. I still do that. If
I don't finish the idea one place, I'll go somewhere else to finish it.

While Disney Hall languished, Gehry received the commission that forever changed his life: the Guggenheim Museum Bilbao. Gehry went to Bilbao first in early 1991 at the invitation of Thomas Krens, longtime director of the Solomon R. Guggenheim Foundation, to give Krens his opinions about the notion of creating a new Guggenheim Museum there. Gehry agreed with Krens that the proposed site didn't work, the two men found another, and after an international competition, Gehry was hired. Early on, says Krens, Gehry's imagery worked—the billowing sails in a maritime setting and the sense of steel that resonated with the industrial history of the Basque Country.

The result is a cultural landmark that the late architect Philip Johnson called "the greatest building of our time." In the ten years after it opened, in October 1997, nearly ten million museum visitors had turned Bilbao into a thriving tourist center. Basque government officials reported the museum generated nearly €1.6 billion during its first ten years.

Krens estimates he has received 130 calls in the last few years to do unto other cities what the Guggenheim Bilbao did unto Bilbao. "Bilbao is a small town, maybe five hundred thousand people," says Krens. "If you put the Guggenheim Bilbao next to the Metropolitan Museum in New York, it is just about as long and 50 percent taller. Imagine that on the edge of Central Park, and here it is in the midst of the Basque Country. If we'd built it at a quarter of its size, it would not have the same impact. Put it at this scale and it's Chartres Cathedral. It's awe-inspiring. Jaw-dropping. No matter how many times people have seen it in photographs, they go there and are stunned by the majesty of it."

BI: How did Bilbao come about?

FG: Tom Krens called me and said the Guggenheim was considering a project in Bilbao and asked me to meet him there. When I arrived, I was shown a beautiful nineteenth-century building in an old neighborhood. It was pretty much gutted, and there were some modern floors with really low ceilings, much like what you'd have in an office building or a hotel. I went through the building with Tom, but he didn't tell me anything; he just showed it to me, and it wasn't very exciting actually.

Afterwards, a group of us all went to dinner at the Lopez de Haro Hotel,

The Guggenheim Bilbao, which opened in 1997, put both the Spanish city of Bilbao and Gehry "on the map," the architect says.

GUGGENHEIM MUSEUM BILBAO, 1997. PHOTO BY DAVID HEALD © THE SOLOMON R. GUGGENHEIM FOUNDATION, NEW YORK

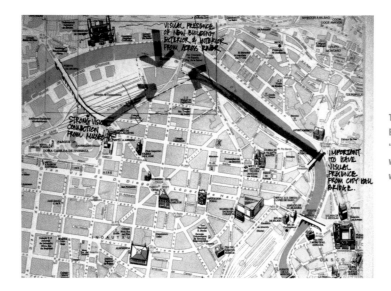

The Guggenheim
Bilbao acquired
"visual presence"
with its busy
waterfront location.

where I ended up spending so much of my life. I was sitting next to Tom, and at one point, somebody stood up, clinked his glass, and said: "We're happy to have Mr. Gehry here, and we'd like to hear from Mr. Gehry what he thinks about our project."

Mr. Gehry just looked at them. They caught me totally off guard—Tom hadn't told me anything, and I hadn't prepared any remarks. But I did have an opinion. So I said, "The problem is that building doesn't lend itself to being a museum. The only way to make it a museum would be to tear down the existing floors and build a new museum inside the walls of the old building. The good news is it would kind of fit in the neighborhood and you'd save the old walls. The bad news is that you would take all the power out of those walls. They would look like a fence. That leads you to the next step, which is to tear down the nineteenth-century façade and build a new museum on the site. The new museum could be beautiful if it's done right, but it would change the whole neighborhood, which now has a certain character. My recommendation is not to do it and to find another site. This site could be easily adapted for use as offices or a hotel, but not for a museum."

BI: How did your hosts react to that?

FG: There was deadly silence. I thought Tom would have kicked me under the table by then, but he didn't. Apparently, my thoughts coincided with what he'd already told them. Later, they took us up on the high wall overlooking the city and asked us where we would put it instead. We showed them where the bridges intersect and the river turns. There's so much stuff happening there already, it would be a great spot.

The Guggenheim Bilbao in context

PHOTO: © ULTAN GUILFOYLE

There was an old brick factory on the site, and the next day they told me it was too expensive and they couldn't get it. So we left, and I thought nothing would happen. I figured that was the end of that. But a few weeks passed, and Tom called to say he wanted me to come back. They had a way to get the site, and he was also interviewing two other architects about it. I agreed to go back, and I took Berta with me, because she speaks Spanish. We had a good time meeting people, and it seemed like they liked us.

BI: So you agreed to participate in a competition?

FG: If it was not a drawn-out competition. I said it's just too hard, and you waste too much money otherwise. This was a three-week competition. They gave each of us ten thousand dollars, and it cost me forty thousand to do it. But we won.

BI: What were your thoughts about Bilbao itself at that point?

FG: Well, I liked Bilbao. I liked the industrial feeling and the surrounding of green, so even though it's a dirty, messy industrial city, it has this forgiveness. The thing I'd like to say about it is that from their standpoint, in hindsight, I was the most conservative choice, even though visually it looked like I wasn't. I was the wild card. As it worked out, had they picked another design, they wouldn't have gotten the public recognition they've gotten.

BI: Juan Ignacio Vidarte, the director of the Guggenheim Bilbao, told me they wanted a building like the Sydney Opera House, which would provide a visual identity and transform the city of Bilbao. How did he and his colleagues express that desire to you?

FG: They said just that: they wanted a Sydney Opera House.

BI: And your reply?

FG: I said, "Well, that's a big order. I can't guarantee anything like that. But I'll do my best."

BI: What led you to design an entrance with wide stairs going down into the museum, rather than going up the way they do nearly everywhere else?

Gehry reaches for his drawing paper and pen.

FG: You have a city at one level, a river at another level, and you're building a three-level museum. If you came in at the middle floor, which is the logical thing to do, you'd have to go up and then down. It would ruin the flow of the museum, because you'd want to see it all in sequence. Sometimes it can work that way, but I thought the river was so beautiful and such an asset that I wanted to make it part of the entry experience. I decided that if you could go down to the river level as the entry point, it could be spectacular. Plus, you'd come in and the atrium could be higher. From an architectural standpoint, it felt better doing that.

It's rarely been done because it feels like you're going down into the basement, so it's a push to get somebody to do that when they're building a fancy building. But we made the entry steps like a big amphitheater, and that's what convinced them that it would work.

It was an interesting problem. All these decisions that seem obvious today weren't obvious at the time. It was a push to do that. There were a lot of questions. Lots of discussions. It was a big deal. But we dogged it through and made it work.

BI: You made another unusual choice in the way museum galleries come off the central atrium rather than lead one into another. My guide at the museum,

Gehry says he designed the Guggenheim Bilbao entry down a wide staircase to maximize its river setting and high atrium.

Maria Bidaurreta, said it had to do with your notions of democracy. She said you felt that that nobody should be forced to go a certain way in a museum.

FG: I probably did say that.

BI: Could you elaborate on that idea?

FG: It was sort of an antidote to the Metropolitan Museum syndrome, where you go in, get lost, and you're there for a few hours with no relief. I like the idea of going to a museum, seeing a section of it, then coming back to the center. You could branch out again, as well as be able to go in a continuous fashion around the central space. In this case, I also wanted to have the central space open to the city so that whenever you came back to that central space, you had different views of the city of Bilbao around you. It made the experience interactive and seeing art interacting with the city made sense to me. The city is a living thing, and the art is inspired by living. It's kind of interrelated.

We just did that at the Art Gallery of Ontario in Toronto, too. It was one of the things that [AGO director] Matthew Teitelbaum wanted. A lot of museum people have picked up on that. It does work. It helps with museum fatigue. And it gives you options. So, in a sense, it *is* democratic.

BI: Much has been said about your choice of titanium for the exterior. How did that come about?

FG: We decided to make the building metal because Bilbao was a steel town, and we were trying to use materials related to their industry. So we built twenty-five mock-ups of a stainless steel exterior with different variations on the theme. But in Bilbao, which has a lot of rain and a lot of gray sky, the stainless steel went dead. It only came to life on sunny days. That's why we could use stainless steel at the Walt Disney Concert Hall in Los Angeles, where there's so much sun it doesn't die.

In order to get life into stainless steel, you can emboss and sand it to get an abrasive quality like [the sculptor] David Smith did. You can David Smith it, where you rough up the surface so it catches the light. That would have worked, but it would have looked like a riff on David Smith. I was frustrated

GUGGENHEIM MUSEUM BILBAO, 1997. PHOTO BY DAVID HEALD © THE SOLOMON R. GUGGENHEIM FOUNDATION, NEW YORK

Gehry chose titanium for the Guggenheim Bilbao for its warmth and ability to go "golden in the gray light."

because nothing was looking right, and I was still struggling with it when I was in my office looking through the sample files. That's where I found a piece of titanium this big.

Gehry makes a square with his hands of about eight inches by eight inches.

BI: What was it about the titanium that caught your eye?

FG: Titanium is buttery. If you look at sterling silver silverware, the knife blade is stainless and the handle is sterling. The sterling silver part looks buttery, just like titanium does, whereas the stainless steel knife blade is cold. I'd also seen big titanium castings made for the 747 airplane, and I remembered

The late critic Herbert Muschamp compared Bilbao's "voluptuous" curves (opposite page) to those of Marilyn Monroe in this 1954 iconic shot during filming of Billy Wilder's *The Seven Year Itch.*

remarking on how buttery they were. They had a warmth to them.

BI: Buttery for you implies warmth?

FG: Yes. Warmth. So I took that piece of titanium, and I nailed it on the telephone pole in front of my office, just to watch it and see what it did in the light. Whenever I went in and out of the office, I'd look at it. As it happened, the day that I tacked it up, it rained in LA, which was unusual, because it wasn't the rainy season. The little metal square went golden in the gray light, and I had another one of those Eureka! moments.

I also liked that titanium had a lot of "oil canning" to it. It had a lot of movement. It wasn't flush and flat.

BI: How would you define "oil canning"?

FG: It's a technical term. Oil canning means that the metal doesn't lie flat. It sort of has shape. Most people don't like it; for years, Richard Meier tried to get rid of oil canning when he was doing metal buildings. But I liked it because of the way it caught the light, which gave it a quality like stone.

I had the guys see if we could get titanium. Well, we found out that titanium was twice the cost of stainless steel and certainly not within our budget. But when I studied the properties of titanium with the people who made it, I found out that it could be half the thickness of stainless. So if you use half the amount of material, you then get it to a price range that's possible.

So the half thickness worked for me. But even at that, the titanium was more expensive than stainless, so we bid it as an alternate. A lot of titanium comes from Russia, and that month the Russians dumped a lot of titanium on the mar-

ket at a low price, so it came in under stainless and we were able to get it and use it. It won't ever happen again, maybe. It just happened by a miracle.

BI: Did you ever imagine the Guggenheim Museum Bilbao would become what it became, in terms of your own career?

FG: Not at all. People were coming by to visit when it was going up; the museum had conferences and all kinds of programming to build up expectations. I guess it did put the city of Bilbao on the map, and I guess it put me on the map. And Disney Hall would not have been built if Bilbao hadn't happened.

BI: Whenever we talk about the Guggenheim Bilbao, I always think of Herbert Muschamp's review in *The New York Times* describing it as a sort of reincarnation of Marilyn Monroe. He said that both stood for an American style of freedom, which he described as "voluptuous, emotional, intuitive and exhibitionist. It is mobile, fluid, material, mercurial, fearless, radiant and as fragile as

Gehry's entryway for the American Center in Paris reminds some people of going under a woman's skirt.

a newborn child. . . . And when the impulse strikes, it likes to let its dress fly up in the air." Were you actually thinking about such things when you were designing the museum?

Gehry, who admired Muschamp and spoke at his memorial gathering, answers a different question.

FG: When I talked at Herbert's memorial, I described how he came to Bilbao and walked the site with me and didn't say very much about whether he liked it or not. But he was aware that artists always have their sexuality stuck right in the middle of their work. I thought that he was trying to understand that in Bilbao and maybe trying to figure me out and get to my sexual triggers. So he used as a metaphor one of the great erotic photographs of our time—Marilyn Monroe with her skirt blowing up—as a way to talk about the sexuality of the building.

BI: But you did have that Monroe picture in your office for a while.

FG: Maybe somebody sent it to me when the review came out?

BI: And all those other images of women that are associated with your buildings?

You told me earlier that your "Fred and Ginger" buildings in Prague were named by someone else, but that's hardly the only example. I've read that the "Miss Brooklyn" building in your Atlantic Yards project was inspired by a Brooklyn bride you saw one day, and a Las Vegas reporter quoted your comments about the lace-petticoat-like roof of your Lou Ruvo Brain Institute there. You've commented publicly on your notion of going under a woman's skirt to enter the American Center building in Paris. That sort of thing.

FG: Well, I say stuff like that after the fact. I don't consciously create a skirt to go under. I think it just comes up and it's obvious. But I'm a guy, and sex and women are on my mind. Sometimes I can help it, but not always. And I'm not the only one who does it. I think there's a lot of sexual energy that goes into the design of a building, and I think it's a good energy. I'm not doing it consciously, but when I see it, I don't edit it out. Let's put it that way. I'm not self-conscious about it.

BI: While we're on the subject, what about the boat imagery that keeps reappearing in your buildings?

FG: I've been interested in sailing since I was in college, and I sailed with other people until I could afford to buy my own boat. I like being out there on the water. It's relaxing. It requires coordination and thinking and keeps your mind active. I like to look at sailboats and regattas, and I like the images of artists like [English romantic painter J. M. W.] Turner and [the maritime painter Willem] Van der Velde. Sails make beautiful spaces. When you have the wind at your back, you put the mainsail out, and then the other, and it creates wing on wing. After I finished Disney Hall, I saw it as wing on wing. But it's never intentional. It's in the DNA.

BI: Does that same theory apply to all your artwork references? Are they intentional? Your design partners cite time after time when you're incorporating art world references in your designs. Edwin Chan said that seeing a show of Matisse cutouts at the Museum of Modern Art sparked some design ideas

VERMEER (VAN DELFT), JAN (1632–1675). *YOUNG WOMAN WITH A WATER PITCHER.* CA. 1662. OIL ON CANVAS, 18 X 16 INCHES. MARQUAND COLLECTION, GIFT OF HENRY G. MARQUAND, 1889 (89.15.21). THE METROPOLITAN MUSEUM OF ART, NEW YORK, NEW YORK, USA. IMAGE © THE METROPOLITAN MUSEUM OF ART/ART RESOURCE, NEW YORK

The pleated headdress in this 1662 Jan Vermeer painting inspired many a Gehry design.

for Bilbao. Craig Webb says your office buildings in Düsseldorf were influenced not just by a Renaissance painting of the Madonna, child, and saints but also by Morandi's bottle villages. Are these influences also after the fact?

Gehry shrugs.

FG: I was very knocked out by the Matisse cutouts, but Morandi was a bigger influence.

BI: I see those Morandi bottles in so many of your designs. Isn't Vermeer also a favorite?

FG: There's a Vermeer painting of a lady with a white shawl that's pleated, and I was inspired by that for Maggie's Centre [the cancer treatment center in Dundee, Scotland, that Gehry designed in honor of his friend Maggie Keswick Jencks, who died from cancer in 1995].

PHOTO: PAUL WARCHOL

Maggie's Centre,
Ninewells Hospital,
Dundee, Scotland,
2003

PHOTO: PAUL WARCHOL

Issey Miyake, flagship store,
New York, New York, 2001

The Jay Pritzker Pavilion,
Millennium Park,
Chicago, 2004

BI: Those pleats reappear in your 2001 titanium sculpture at Issey Miyake's Tribeca-based store in downtown New York. Miyake is well known for his fabric pleating, and his associate Jun Kanai told me you talked with her about doing something else with Miyake's pleats, too.

FG: I did. I didn't start out to do it, but look at the Pritzker Pavilion I did in Chicago [at the Millennium Park in 2004]. I told Issey that it was like his pleats. Again, I might have been influenced, but I wasn't consciously inspired by them. Those referents always come out after the fact. When I saw those pleats at the Pritzker, I said, "Oh my God, look at that. There are pleats."

PART 3 · CONSOLIDATING

Gehry's sketch and Sydney Pollack's photograph highlight the Guggenheim Bilbao in context.

EVERYTHING CHANGED after Bilbao, including Los Angeles roadblocks to Disney Hall. Asked what stopped Disney Hall construction earlier, the Los Angeles Philharmonic's former executive director, Ernest Fleischmann, suggests, "It was probably because at the time Frank got Disney Hall, his office was small. He didn't have enough staff to do the working drawings. The executive architect appointed to do it couldn't produce working drawings based on Gehry's design." When "the Bilbao effect" boosted Gehry's staff pool as well as his reputation, says Fleischmann, Gehry's office was able to take over the working drawings.

Technology has been a boon to architecture generally and Gehry specifically, allowing not just more wondrously curved exteriors for buildings but also more control for architects. The CATIA computer system developed for the Mirage fighter plane was reconfigured for Gehry buildings and has become a crucial tool in contemporary architectural practice. Next door to the Gehry Partners office is Gehry Technologies, the computer design spinoff he launched in 2002, which is already operating internationally. "Complicated buildings like Disney Hall could be designed and working drawings produced that would give confidence to the contractors doing the building," says Richard Koshalek, chair of the hall's architectural selection subcommittee. "Architects are now intricately involved in construction to a degree they never were before and have greater authority and control over the architecture process itself."

Of late, Gehry has also given more attention to his legacy. As he designs new buildings and projects around the world, he continues to influence the ideas and futures of countless younger architects. He has taught generations of architects at Yale, Harvard, UCLA, and elsewhere, and the list of distinguished architects who moved on from his office is a long one.

With new designs and new buildings regularly in the news, he is more confident and clear about what he will and will not do. "Bilbao has been the watershed thing for Frank," observes Thomas Krens. "He was an interesting architect until Bilbao opened. After that, he became a transcendent architect."

As Gehry has become even more of a public figure, each project seems more high-profile than the last. During just two weeks in October 2006, he received global coverage—including three New York Times articles—for the Louis Vuitton Foundation for Creation in Paris, the Hotel Marqués de Riscal—a new luxury hotel in Spain—and the future expansion of the Philadelphia Museum of Art.

BI: How has your architecture practice changed since Bilbao?

FG: Since Bilbao, clients who hire us have an aspiration to do something special. They saw the Bilbao effect, as it's called, which is a compelling argument. Clients have a vision of what they need and want, and when they hire architects from among the twenty or thirty high-powered top designers in the world, they do it because they want something special.

There is the occasional client who doesn't give a damn. That client just wants to build something, and a lot of that is also happening now. But I think that's a different model.

BI: If you received a call on a project like that, would you be interested?

FG: I don't think so. I'm old-fashioned.

BI: In director Lyndel King's office at the Weisman Museum in Minneapolis, I saw a framed sketch of the museum you'd sent her that was inscribed "It takes a great client." What makes a great client for you?

FG: I've got to choose wisely when they come at me, especially now. When I was younger, I took my chances and tried to help mold a client into a good client. Tom Krens is a genius. He has a vision. He's got an ego, and he's got his own thing, and he's fun to play with. He energizes me. I energize him. We inspire each other. And you can feel it. It's exhilarating when you work with him.

BI: You have referred in the past to Bruce Ratner, the New York developer on Atlantic Yards, as a good client.

FG: Bruce is a very well educated guy. I don't have to teach him the importance of art. He's committed. You can be open about what your intentions are and what you're trying to achieve. He can't afford to build something that will be a negative business deal, of course. So he's trying to navigate the relationship between what I do and what they have done, between the commercial enterprise and Bruce and my architectural aspirations. It's been a learning curve. We have both been working at it, diligently, and having that kind of relationship is important to me.

BI: You always refer to architecture as a service business.

FG: I've always thought about architecture that way. You get a client, and that client may be one person or a group of people. The client needs a building, and you design, produce, and deliver it. You try to be within their budget, serve their purpose, and solve their problem. There is a responsibility beyond that to the community, both the community close in and the community at large, and this is something on which architects are idealistic. They feel like their contributions to the community are going to make a difference in the character, life, and identity of the community. If it's a nice building and people identify with it, as happened at Bilbao, it becomes a part of the community and has an emotional role in the community. In recent times, things like energy savings and "green architecture" have become more and more important to address, in Europe especially because the laws require it more than they do in America.

BI: And your own creative needs? How do they fit in the puzzle?

FG: For my own gratification, I have a need to grow, so that I'm not repeating myself, and to try and establish, in the context of all that went before, a better product.

In other words, there's a tendency to want to better yourself. In some cases, architects may take a language they've invented and use it for their whole lifetime; Mies van der Rohe was that kind of architect, and he was damn good, so that's not by necessity a bad thing. I'm more like Eero Saarinen. Saarinen used to try to explore different techniques, and I have those tendencies. Le Corbusier showed me how he worked out his architectural language and his buildings in paintings.

No matter what you build, after you solve all the issues of function and budget and so on, you bring to it your language, your signature of some sort, and I think that's important. The most important thing is to be yourself, because as soon as you try to be somebody else, you tend to denigrate the work and it's not as powerful or as strong. I always tell my students that they should be themselves, because when you are yourself, you're the expert on you. You're the only expert, and that's a nice place to be.

I also know that if I take a project on other terms than mine, for me it will fail. It will be a fight all the way through. I'm in the fortunate position now of being able to walk away from that.

BI: And before you were so prominent?

FG: I don't know if it's the same for everybody, but when I started out, I seemed a little more conservative. Then I hit the roadblock of bad construction workmanship in the sixties, and I took the fork in the road to expose the wood, rough framing and all that, and to make a virtue out of it. That's when I started using corrugated metal and plywood. I went through that period, and then I got better jobs, better projects, and better budgets. You couldn't not know what Robert Venturi was doing, or what Richard Meier was doing, and I would see the work of my contemporaries, but I really followed my own nose. I always kept to my own kind of language.

BI: Did you question where that individualism was taking you?

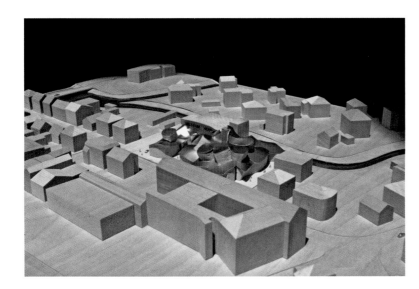

Gehry Partners makes models of future buildings in context with their neighbors.

FG: No. I learned the lesson as a kid that you should never talk down to people. I think my mother taught me that when we were living in Canada and there were a lot of foreigners there. You know how people talk to foreigners in pidgin English? People around us were always doing that, and my mother didn't like that. And I feel the same thing in architecture. You should never talk down to people with your work. You should always assume that they understand.

You can do the equivalent of pidgin English by designing dumb, simple buildings that you know people will understand and like, and that seems to me

to be talking down to people. You don't know whether you're talented or not. You don't know whether you're any good or not. You just think you must do this stuff, and you do it. If people like it, you're lucky. But not everybody will like it. The same number of people are going to hate it and like it, so you might as well do the best you can and let it go. That's what I do.

An assistant enters with a photo.

FG: The latest from the front. It's a nice little building. The MARTa Herford museum [of contemporary art and design] in Herford, Germany. See how nice it fits . . .

BI: Making it a good example of how you don't design buildings in isolation.

FG: The way we work is we make models of the context that the buildings are going to be in. We pretty thoroughly document it because that gives me visual clues. For instance, in Herford I wandered around the streets, and I found that all the public buildings were brick and all the private buildings were plaster. Since this is a public building, I decided to make it brick, because that's the language of the town. I also had models of the existing buildings, so that when I put the new building into the site model, I could see that it was going to be a comfortable fit in the neighborhood. It wasn't going to be too big, and it wasn't going to be too small. It was going to be just right. Mama Bear, Papa Bear, and Baby Bear. I really spend time doing that, and if you go to Bilbao, you'll see that even though the building looks pretty exuberant, it is very carefully scaled to what's around it.

Gehry is lost in the photograph in his hand. He can't take his eyes off it.

FG: I'm really proud of this one.

BI: We've talked briefly about how good a building looks, before you put the skin on it, and this would be an example. Is there a thrill to seeing that?

FG: At this point, there is an excitement about the way it looks. I haven't been over there for a while, and the photographs suggest that it's coming out

PHOTO: THOMASMAYERARCHIVE.COM

Frank Gehry works with wood models in his office.

pretty well. But I always have trepidation. Not everything can go perfectly, so there are going to be some mistakes that I'm going to get upset about when I get there. There will be my mistakes, and there may be mistakes by other people. There's a lot of press written that refers to my work as an ego trip, and that the architecture is too loud for the art. I don't relate much to any of that because I really love art a lot, and I've spent a lot of time with artists and for the most part I take good care of them with my buildings. I have gotten a lot of feedback from them that they like what I'm doing. So this other argument is sort of a cheap shot from visually illiterate curators and museum directors who are afraid. Their defense is to say those things about me.

BI: Do you have a favorite time when you're working on a building?

FG: Yes. It's when I have the plans and the scale right for both the neighborhood and the project in block form, before I make these curved shapes, before I do anything. When I get to that point, I feel comfortable that this is where we're going to go, and the next move is just to finish the detailing, materials, and character of the shapes. It's what I call being in the candy store, because that's the fun part. It's also the most scary part because it's the unknown. I start sketching and trying things until, all of a sudden, something emerges that becomes interesting and I sort of follow it. But it's intuitive. It's not preconceived. I don't have an exact plan of action, and I always feel like I'm leaping off a cliff.

BI: Do you feel like you're taking your collaborators with you?

FG: I collaborate with people on projects because it enriches the mix and gets you somewhere else that you wouldn't have gotten to otherwise. When it's really working, it is like holding hands and jumping off a cliff together.

BI: Do you think perfection is possible?

FG: At the University of Southern California, they had cut in stone above the door a quote from Michelangelo which said, "A work of art is but a shadow of the divine perfection." I like that because it got me off the hook.

BI: You may not go after perfection, but you often refer to a job well done as appearing to be "a magic trick." What do you mean by that?

FG: Magic for me is when all of the ideas, all of the thoughts, all of the time devoted to realizing a project come together and produce something that the world thinks is beautiful.

BI: How often does that happen?

FG: It doesn't happen often. We're lucky when it happens, and we should hope for it.

BI: How does the notion of creating a sense of place fit into all this?

FG: I think creating a sense of place is one of the most important issues facing an architect. And if you fail, you'll find out quickly because people won't go there.

BI: We haven't talked much about mentors.

FG: Well, Philip Johnson was certainly a mentor. I was attracted to Philip because he was an art collector, and I didn't know many architects who were art collectors. Artists and other friends told me that when he was ready, Philip would come. Philip came to see the Ron Davis house, and later he asked me to call him if I ever came east. He was very nice to me and very friendly. And then I started doing a house for Christophe de Menil, and she knew Philip, of course, because he did her mother Dominique's house, so we would get together. When I was teaching at Yale, I used to invite Philip to my juries, and he would invite me to dinner when I was in New York. We became friends, and whenever he was in Los Angeles, he would come visit.

BI: He also brought the whole architecture community closer, didn't he?

FG: Yes. He loved architects, and he loved architecture. He spent a lot of time and effort to help younger architects like Michael Graves. He helped Peter Eisenman many times. He helped a lot of people.

They used to have the roundtable at the Century Club where architects were invited. I stopped going a long time ago. At some point it became sado-masochistic because they'd bring you in, then go around the table and every-body would say something about your work and you'd have to defend yourself. It was a question of who could be the most honest, and it wasn't easy to do.

BI: Did they treat you like the out-of-towner?

PHOTO: © ULTAN GUILFOYLE

Sydney Pollack interviews Philip Johnson for Pollack's film *Sketches of Frank Gehry.*

FG: For a while they did, yes. And Philip was brutally frank with people. He would say exactly what was on his mind, and I found that very refreshing when it came to my work. I know other people squirmed, but I liked it. It made you think. Sometimes I didn't agree with him, and I was comfortable with that, too. He didn't demand obeisance. When we did the Beverly Hills Civic Center competition, several of us showed our plans to him, and he was brutal to each of us. He didn't like our plans. He thought they were really not very good. And he was right.

BI: You don't enter competitions much anymore, do you?

FG: Disney Hall was a competition. Bilbao was a competition.

BI: But those are a while ago. I mean now.

FG: No, not too often. The only time we enter them now is when we get caught by friends who are doing things and want us to, but I try to stay out of it. If you can get work from people who come to you because they want you, you have a better chance of doing good work. They know what they want, and the relationship is much stronger from the beginning.

In a competition, you don't know the people, and if you win, you're in a room with a bunch of people who liked one of the other schemes. There's a lot of equivocating. I think if you can get work directly, it's got a greater chance of being better, and the experience of doing it will be less toxic.

BI: Are there commissions or projects you would like to do that you haven't gotten?

FG: I'm superstitious about that, so I don't covet anything. There's something that prevents me from yearning for a project. I guess I don't like the disappointment. I could say I want to do an airport, because I like flying. I worked on LAX, the Los Angeles airport, years ago, and I have ideas about airports. It's a complicated mechanism, and I think I could do something interesting. But between wanting to do it and getting a commission, there are a lot of hoops you need to jump through and so I sort of wait. If somebody has an airport they want me to do, then I'll do it, but I'm not going to go begging for an airport. The projects I do are the ones that come in the door and hit me over the head.

I have friends who go after things, and they get a lot of nice work. When I was younger, I might have done it, and if work stopped coming to me, I might be forced to do that. I'm not holier-than-thou about it. I don't think it's a bad thing to do, and I don't necessarily think you're degrading yourself to do it. It's just nicer if you don't have to.

BI: The Fishdance Restaurant you did in Kobe in the mid-eighties was a competition, wasn't it? The client asked you to do a fish, right? It wasn't your idea?

FG: That's true. I went to Kobe to see the site, and the client took me out to dinner. They got me sake'd up, and they asked me to do sketches on napkins, which other architects had also done for them. I drew little boxes, things like this . . .

Gehry reaches for his pen and paper and starts sketching. When he's done, he first holds the sketch in his hand appreciatively, then shows it to me.

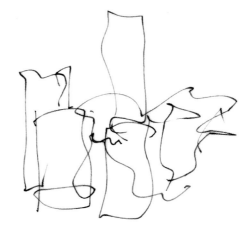

Gehry drew an "anything" on a paper napkin, launching his participation in a competition to design the Fishdance Restaurant in Kobe, Japan.

BI: What is it?

FG: I don't know what it is. They asked me to do drawings on napkins, and that's what I did.

BI: Drawings of anything.

FG: Yes. I did drawings of anythings. Then they said, "Gehry-san, make a fish drawing."

More sketching.

And I did this. *Mira!* Look what I did. Fish on waves. Then I went home, and three weeks from that day, they sent me a note saying, "Congratulations. You won the competition." I didn't have a clue that there was any kind of competition.

Then they sent me a set of architectural drawings for a building that looked like my napkin sketch. I told them, "We can't build that. There are typhoon winds in Kobe. A typhoon will shake the fish on top and break the glass under it." They said, "No, it will work." I said, "Show me." So they left. I think in between I did one or two studies, but they didn't like them. I was trying to show them how to do it by separating the pieces, and they said they didn't like it. They only liked the one that they sent me drawings for.

Do you understand what they did? They took my napkin sketch, interpreted it by themselves, brought it to me and said, "This is the building." I told them technically it can't work. I was happy to make a building that looked like that. That was fine. It was like a big fish lamp, and I would have had a lot of fun with it. But I couldn't make it work.

So they went away. A while later, they called me on a Friday night. It was Saturday afternoon in Japan, and they were telling me, "Gehry-san, we have a serious problem. We cannot make the building work." I said, "Fine, so let me design it now finally," and they said, "Yes, please." I said, "I'll call you tomorrow and give you a schedule. I need two or three months to study it." They replied that they needed a design by Monday. I said, "I can't do it. I'm sorry."

They hung up, and I was so upset, I couldn't get to sleep that night. My first job in Japan, right? I was very disappointed. Then at 4 a.m., they called again, and they made it very clear to me how important it was for them to have me do it and to do it fast. So I went to the office the next day, we worked on a design and on Sunday morning we sent Greg Walsh to Japan with drawings and models.

BI: Greg Walsh says he must have made ten trips to Kobe on this project, going back and forth, trying to make their deadline.

FG: He stayed there on and off a long time and helped them. We also faxed back and forth—there was no e-mail then—and we developed the project by fax and phone and models, over the next two or three weeks. The fish tail was the hardest thing to do, and we made a separate model for that. But when we sent that model to Japan, it got damaged in transit, sort of cracked, and that's the way they built it. They built it like the model. I wanted to light it from the outside, to keep the form, but they didn't like that because they had a fish lamp in mind. They wanted to light it from the inside, and see the whole structure. We liked each other, but there was a real lack of communication. You could never get traction with them. So from start to finish, the whole building was a complete misunderstanding.

BI: Situations like that sound so frustrating. How do you manage to keep inspiration going when you're engulfed in that sort of thing?

FG: I tell my students when you're stuck, go to a museum. I do it myself. I'll go to a museum and look at a painting, and that always uncorks me. I'll always find something in the painting. I do it with literature a bit, too, and with music. Concerts make me explode with ideas. It's just uncontrollable. Sometimes I can't even focus on the music, I get so carried away. But the best trigger for me is going to the museum.

BI: Is it a particular artist or painting or type of art?

FG: Usually the trigger for me is looking at ancient art. Early stuff. Also, Picasso. Matisse. Rodin.

DWGS FOR NAPKINS
WITH FISH DANCE CLIENTS
BEFORE STARTING DESIGN
PROCESS

FISH DANCE RESTAURANT
PD INTERPRETED BY
JAPANESE CLIENT
AFTER NAPKIN SKETCH

FISH DANCE
RESTAURANT

RESTAURANT
ALA ROOM
DROWS

SNAKE

FISH

3 PIECE FISH DANCE
VILLAGE

Sketches, a model, and a photograph of the Fishdance Restaurant in
Kobe, Japan

BI: We've talked about Carl Andre, Rauschenberg, and Rembrandt. Are there others who come to mind?

FG: Well, I look at a lot of work. A few years ago, when [the art historian] Irving Lavin introduced me to [fourteenth-century Flemish sculptor] Claus Sluter, I went gaga. When I looked at the Van der Velde sailing pictures, same thing. Orozco.

BI: You've named both painters and sculptors. Does sculpture have a particular attraction for you?

FG: Yes, but painting more. Sculpture is more definite. Painting is more ephemeral, so you can read more into it. You're freer to interpret from paintings than you are from a 3-D object. You can fantasize more. It's not that the images you're looking at are translatable into a building; it's the fact that the images are there and they're so beautiful. They're so filled with ideas. What I get out of it probably has nothing to do with the painting, except for the energy of it. Knowing that some human being got revved up and did it, revs me up to do something.

BI: Does nature do that for you, too? Looking at the ocean, looking at a mountain . . .

FG: All of that. Animals do, too. The shells of turtles. The fish lamps and snakes and all of that came from nature. My old house and my new house are both very much involved with nature.

BI: Your creative stimuli seem to come from everywhere.

FG: They do. It comes from the people who I work with, the clients, the environment, and the hopes and aspirations of the projects I work on. I have to feel politically and socially attuned to them to respond with creative energy, to get excited, to want to do it.

BI: What about instinct?

FG: I find something and I tend to poke at it, like a cat pokes at something. I'm curious. As I said earlier, I think it's important to learn to trust one's instincts. I always say that if I knew in advance where I was going, I wouldn't go there. So I'm constantly letting things just evolve in response to a problem.

BI: You've often talked of how you use the energy of others to fuel your own.

FG: When I was a kid, I studied jujitsu, and then, much later, karate. Jujitsu is interesting because opponents come at you, and you use their energy to overwhelm them. You take the energy that they supply to the event to contain them, and I find that's true in creative working, too. You can sometimes turn those kinds of assaults in the working relationship to accept the challenge and then take charge of it, so to speak, using the energy of the people who are trying to mess with you.

There are two kinds of energy. There's the energy that probably comes from my mother pushing me for many years to do something, and I guess I'm afraid to disappoint her even though she's gone. She's the only one I ever sent clippings to. But there's also the energy of the work that grows out of the excitement of the project. A lot has to do with the people involved and their willingness to play with me. I think the best buildings come out of that.

BI: How do you define play?

FG: Creative play is childlike. It's questioning. It's fun. Well, it's partly fun. It's looking for something. You don't know what. And in architecture, you're doing it with a lot of other people.

BI: Do images and ideas come to you in dreams as well?

FG: I do have dream images but they're not in sound sleep. They're just before I fall asleep. When I'm thinking of a project, I'll vividly see the answer—the building, the form. They're very vivid pictures. I'm not totally asleep, and I can remember them the next morning.

BI: Maybe it's the silence.

FG: Silence is good. It's something we don't get much of. It allows your thinking processes to free-range, when you're not being bombarded with a lot of ambient noise. It's harder and harder to find silence. Think about the library and how you go to the library for quiet, then start free-associating with books. It's expansive, and no matter who you are, moments in a quiet environment are cherished moments.

In negotiations, it's better to listen. I think lawyers do that. Some people come in and just start talking and then they don't listen to what the other person is worried about. But it's good to listen and use what you hear, not necessarily against them, but as a way of engaging. People getting together and agreeing on things is complicated because some people feel like their contribution is bigger than the other person, or they feel insecure and their contribution isn't bigger, but they want it to be. It's really hard, and in the end these things escalate and become wars. I'm not that kind of a fighter.

I don't like to argue with people, so I try to put my conditions out quickly. That way, people understand what I'm sensitive to, and then they have something to deal with. You can also say nothing, just be a sphinx and then people don't know what you're thinking. You may win that way, but the relationships get tangled and anxiety-filled, and I try to avoid that. As I'm getting older, I *really* try to avoid it. As soon as something gets like that, I will walk away.

BI: You say yes to a great many projects. Isn't your attention split in a million directions?

FG: Working on one single project is something I've always found difficult. I need a little pressure and to work on lots of things at once. I get energy from working. You need a mix to bounce off. It's like billiards. I need three or four projects at least, so that I don't overthink one of them.

I also like the energy things give to each other. If you're doing one thing and something happens to it—if the building department or the client decides to stop things—you're desperate. Over the years, I've always tried to be doing a bunch of things so that I feel more secure. They're not all going to go away at once.

BI: Have you ever had everything go away at once?

FG: Yes, in 1978. I had done a lot of work for the Rouse Company, and most of the people in my office were working on Rouse projects. Matt DeVito, the president of Rouse, came out for the opening of Santa Monica Place [shopping mall]. Since we were friends, I invited him home for dinner. He looked at my house, with its chain link and other nontraditional building materials, in its first iteration, much rougher than it is now, and he thought it was pretty strange. During dinner, he said, "You must like this. You did it for yourself." I said, "I do." Pointing in the direction of Santa Monica Place, he asked, "If you like this, how could you like *that*?" So I said, "Well, I don't." When he asked, "Then why did you do it?" I told him, "I have to make a living." He said he didn't think I should do work I didn't want to do. I agreed, we shook hands, and we agreed that we would quit working together.

That was on a Friday night, and on Monday, I had to go to the office and let nearly everybody go. I had about fifty people working there. I kept three. I asked Berta to come in, because we didn't have a receptionist or anything. It was an emergency, so she dug in and did it. She became our chief financial officer out of that.

So I've seen that devil. That wasn't the first time something like that has happened either. It happened earlier, and it's happened since.

BI: I know there have been several projects that have been planned but not built, but have you ever again walked away like that?

FG: Once I'm committed to a project, I'll finish it because it's fair to do so. But in the case of Rouse, there was the president of the company sitting with me and telling me, "Look, let's not do this. It's bad for both of us," and he was right. So we stopped by mutual agreement. I didn't leave him high and dry, and there were no projects that I left unfinished.

But since that point, I won't let any one client account for more than 50 percent of our work at one time. I try to keep that figure down to around 40 percent, and it's better if it's 35 percent, because things happen on both sides. It's not good for them, and it's not good for me.

BI: How do you keep that percentage down? For instance, it looks to me like you're doing a lot of work now for Bruce Ratner. Besides Atlantic Yards,

Gehry has designed the Beekman Tower (center) in lower Manhattan.

there's the Beekman apartment tower you designed for him in lower Manhattan, near the Brooklyn Bridge.

FG: Between the Brooklyn project and the Beekman Tower, our work with Bruce was growing over the 35 percent level, so I took in more work. That's why the office tends to get bigger. That's the only way to do it. You're not going to turn down good projects.

BI: Does this upset Ratner or your other clients?

FG: This is not done behind their backs. They understood. They agreed with it. They had other work to give us, but we backed off.

BI: Do you have other rules like that?

FG: As you know, I started with not a lot of money and from the beginning I wouldn't borrow money. That philosophy began when I opened my office in

1962, and I've kept that rule pretty intact. Over all these years, maybe we've borrowed money three times and only when payments were late and I knew it was just for a short time. That meant I had to work within our fees, whatever they were, and at the beginning they weren't very big. I'd work day and night, doing most of the work.

BI: That surely isn't the case anymore. Every time I come by here, there seem to be not just more models but more desks, more computers, more people. They also seem to be getting younger and younger and less and less familiar to me.

FG: We have turnover at the lower level, which is both logical and important. Talented young designers come in, and if they stay too long, they get hooked into my thing, so I talk to them about it. It's not a hidden agenda. They tell me their dreams of opening their own offices, and I act accordingly. After about four or five years, I usually say they should be thinking about going their own way. And if they want to stay, they can. Edwin Chan and Craig Webb have stayed, and they now do a lot of the design work with me.

Gehry works with design partner
Edwin Chan.

BI: How many projects would you personally be involved with at any given time, and how many might the office be involved with?

FG: Well, it's not like that. I'm involved in everything, but it goes through phases. In the early phase, schematics and design development, I'm very involved. When the projects go into production, I'm less involved, and when they go into construction, I'm less involved except to answer questions and to deal with aberrant changes or conditions. I always have to make adjustments in the field, so I do that. There are maybe four or five in the design phase at one time and maybe a total of twenty projects in various phases. I may be involved with ten projects right now, but five of them are intense. Then, as those drift out, the other five that I'm involved in will become more intense and by that time there will be five more.

BI: You and other architects are always referring to your designers in terms of teams. What's this notion of "the design team"?

FG: I'm a big sports nut. I go to the gym every morning. I played hockey. And the way I talk about the office is that it's like a basketball game. If I give an idea to the guys, they pop it back to me fast. Then we develop a rhythm of working, and we can explore a lot of ideas together quickly.

Gehry works with design partner Craig Webb.

The design evolves in a process in which they participate. They can watch it evolving and they know they're part of it. You know, I don't sit in a room and design a building and then say, "This is it, client." It evolves from the inside out. So I have developed a way of working with the staff that allows me to delegate, which is one of the hardest things for somebody to do who has a single-minded design language. I don't keep that creative process private. I think there are people who guard their privacy in their creative work, who go somewhere alone and think it through and come back with it.

BI: You do both, don't you?

FG: I do the dream and I do the drawings, but I never get too far away from the men and women here. We're trying to bring more women up in design. Ours is a typical male chauvinist pig office, although we don't intend it to be that way, of course. It has not been easy keeping women.

BI: How do you keep track of all these projects?

FG: Each project has somebody in charge, and I meet with those people. They usually e-mail and say they need me and we set up a time. When there's a heavy design issue, then I'll sit down for the whole day with them and really slug it through until we get somewhere. I pretty much stay out of the business stuff. I do the big-picture business stuff but not the details.

BI: What about choosing your clients and projects? Is there ever a time when you work on a project and then decide you don't want to do it?

FG: Yes. But you have to do it right at the beginning, because as soon as you commit to a client, it's expensive for them if you unhook. So you've really got to analyze projects well. That's what we do at our partners' meetings. We take all the projects that have come in, and we discuss the pros and cons together.

BI: How often do you meet?

FG: We try to meet once a week, but there are so many people traveling that we have trouble getting them all together.

BI: Speaking of travel, it seems you're always either just back from somewhere or about to go somewhere else.

Gehry goes over to his desk and picks up a very small, very used datebook and starts reading aloud. He talks about a presentation in London, a meeting in Paris, another in Basel. Flipping a few pages, he calls out more dates, more projects, more cities, more countries. New York. Boston. Venice.

BI: A schedule like that would be difficult in your fifties or sixties, much less your seventies.

FG: It is hard. I think about it all the time, and I worry about it. I'm not looking forward to getting on a plane tomorrow night to Hong Kong, but it's become a way of life.

BI: Do you keep a suitcase packed?

FG: No, but I can pack in five minutes. I wear T-shirts and jackets. I'm not a fancy dresser, so it doesn't matter. I bring along drawing paper, and sometimes I'll sketch. I usually carry a traditional book and a Books on Tape recording, and I'll do both, plus I usually read three or four magazines on a trip and all the newspapers. I don't watch television much in hotels. I just put the TV on when I'm going to bed because it puts me to sleep. I might buy a movie off the TV or something, but that's rare. They really have junk on television.

I usually have dinner with clients. Even in New York, where I have a lot of friends, I don't call them very much. We keep the trips as tight as we can, so most of the dinners aren't social. When I was younger I used to see all the architects, but everybody is so competitive, I decided to forget it. I would say my time in New York now is quite low-key, uneventful, mostly business-oriented. In Europe I see Rolf Fehlbaum all the time. Rolf owns Vitra, my first building in Europe, and we're doing some furniture with him.

BI: Do you take the weekends off?

FG: Sunday I usually take off. And we have a fairly constant evening demand. We have three business dinners a week, probably.

BI: You chose a very demanding career, didn't you?

FG: Well, it takes up all your time. You don't have much time for other things. I've got two boys who I spend a lot of time with, and when I'm in town, Berta and I try to spend as many evenings at home as we can. But that's not always successful. I don't get to see a lot of friends. I often get stuck with something and have to cancel and I hate that.

BI: The logical next question is—

FG: How do I do it?

BI: Exactly.

FG: I don't know. If I find out, I may not want to know. It would scare me.

BI: Let's look at it another way then. Given the number of things you're doing, how do you prioritize your time?

FG: Obviously, there's the family priority. Family is the best thing you ever do. It's very complicated, but it's worth doing. I struggle with how to help my kids, and I spend a lot of my time worrying and thinking about them. There's the work priority, Gehry Partners, and secondary to that, the various products I'm working on. After that, everything else sort of plays second fiddle, because if there's a time crunch it goes to Gehry Partners and to the family.

BI: How much do you sleep?

FG: Seven hours. I get up at 6:30.

BI: How do you get started?

FG: I go to the gym and I have breakfast. I get back at 9:30, quarter to ten, read *The New York Times* and the *Los Angeles Times* and go to the office. Usually while I'm driving back and forth to places, I'm on the phone with the office; they plug me into phone calls to people trying to get me. And then we e-mail constantly.

The hardest thing, the thing that throws everything off, is the travel. That's the monkey wrench. We're not so wealthy that we can afford a company jet, which would make things a little bit easier. Nonstop planes help. When there's a crisis and I have to get somewhere, most of my clients will spring for a private plane to take me.

BI: You've done some flying, haven't you?

FG: I sit in the cockpit sometimes. I do know how to do it, a little bit. Like everything else I do, I'm a dilettante. Except for architecture.

BI: How does fame affect all of this?

FG: Well, I don't know what to make of fame. I see somebody like Brad Pitt, who I know, and what he goes through, and I wouldn't want to go through that. He's so young and his personal life is so scrutinized. I only get maybe 1 percent of that and it's scary already.

BI: But there's also that substantial upside to fame.

FG: You do want people to hear about you, and come to you with work. There's nothing complicated about that. So you've got to get known somehow, for something, and hopefully you get known for doing good work, and then that's the reason. I've tried to keep it at that level, and try to do good work. One of my college teachers told me that whatever you do, no matter how small, just give it the best you can because you're only as good as your last project. If you throw in the towel on something because it's hard, you pay dearly for it, and the word gets out quickly.

So I've always tried to make it the best I could and give people their money's worth. That leads to some notoriety, called fame, and then if you do good work, the press wants to hear about it. If the project is of a public nature, people want to read about it. If it's good, you get a lot of action. Part of it is natural and part of it is contrived. Clients hire publicists, which is their right, and we participate. Willingly. We don't usually refuse that when it's a client unless it's something I don't want to do, in which case I'll tell the client and give them good reasons.

BI: And the criticism that comes with all that recognition?

FG: Some of it is pretty harsh, but I'm sort of used to it. If you read the good stuff, you have to be willing to read the bad stuff as well, so sometimes it's better not to read any of it. But when it's bad, even if you didn't read it, people tell you, sometimes with great glee. But that's all right. Our culture is like that, so I think you have to expect it and live with it and not complain.

BI: Is there an advantage to achieving fame when you're older?

FG: My experience with friends who became famous in younger years was that it was really difficult for them to sustain. I feel blessed that whatever fame I've gotten came when I was in my sixties and seventies, so if it looks like it's going the other way, I can gracefully retire.

MIXING IT UP WITH GENIUSES

ithin a year of the Bilbao opening, Gehry began work on the Ray and Maria Stata Center for Computer, Information, and Intelligence Sciences at the Massachusetts Institute of Technology. Expected to open in 2003 (it actually opened in the spring of 2004), it was to be twice the size of the Guggenheim Bilbao and replace MIT's fabled Building 20, where radar was developed during World War II. The high-profile project was the crown of a 2001 Frank Gehry retrospective at the Guggenheim Museum in New York—the most popular show in the Guggenheim's history—and filled the top floor of Frank Lloyd Wright's museum with Stata models, drawings, photos, and other materials. Gehry and I talked about that project first for an article which appeared in Esquire *magazine in July 2001, and which is when most of the following conversation took place. We revisited Stata in 2007, when it was again in the news for very different reasons.*

BI: How would you describe the Stata Center project at MIT?

FG: It's close to 430,000 square feet of space. When it's done, it will include three different labs, offices, and other requirements for faculty and students, as well as communal spaces like a café, library, child-care center, meeting rooms, and lecture halls. There are also shops for various and sundry things and parking in the basement.

It's not a very complicated "program" or assignment. It's just that the people using it are complicated. Since they're in science, they need a lot of flexibility. They need a building that's changeable, very quickly, and adaptable because they start down one track and often end up going down another.

BI: Were you familiar with the MIT campus?

A sketch, a model, and a photograph of the Stata Center at MIT

FG: I was. When I was at Harvard Graduate School of Design in the 1950s, I took some classes at MIT. Because I lived in Cambridge, I walked around there a lot. Later, I also taught design at MIT.

BI: Do you remember your interview at MIT for this job?

FG: There was a presentation about the campus design, which included an explanation, in great detail, of what an architect should understand about MIT and where it was going. When it was over, I was asked my opinion, and I said, "I think that direction is doomed to failure. I think it doesn't have anything to do with the present, and with all due respect, I think it's the wrong way to go." I couldn't help it. I had to say what I thought because I didn't want to go in under false pretenses.
Then they selected us.

BI: Isn't there more to this story? For instance, before they selected you, didn't they come out and look around your office?

FG: Yes. They sent out their senior scientists; all these high-powered brains visited my office, and they were impressive, by God. I showed them what I do and how I do it.

BI: What do you think they took away from seeing this office of yours?

The Stata Center succeeded MIT's historic Building 20, which was built during World War II and where radar was developed.

FG: Well, this is not a buttoned-down corporate office. It's like an artist's studio. Models all over the place. It's worked in. Lived in. It's very humanistic, I would say. I think people find it user-friendly, which was like the environments they wanted. No fussy details, just warm wood and warm humanistic spaces that were quasi-industrial. I find compulsive, perfect detailing to be incompatible with the lives we're now leading. To me it suggests aloofness and pretension. While a lot of people, especially wealthy people, like this kind of anal-compulsive perfection in architecture, I've always felt that was irrelevant. If you go to Bilbao, the detailing is not precious. It's very matter-of-fact. But having said that, it takes as much time to design matter-of-fact detailing as it does to make precious detailing.

BI: What did you learn from them, in turn? Since this building would be incorporating their historic Building 20, did you know much about Building 20 at that point?

FG: I knew radar was developed there, and I knew that Noam Chomsky worked there. I'd seen the building, which looked like an old army barracks. The scientists liked it because they could go in and bang holes in the walls and put up cable trays wherever they wanted. They didn't feel like it was "architecture" that they had to respect and be deferential to. It was a building that served their impulses and their feelings, and they resisted tearing it down.

BI: But it was meant to be temporary, wasn't it?

FG: Yes. It was meant to be temporary, although it lasted fifty-five years. But it had asbestos in the walls so it really didn't merit saving. They would be stuck with something that was a historic icon, but an albatross in terms of their lives.

BI: So Building 20 was torn down.

FG: Yes. I've got a piece of it that they gave to me in the office, and as I design their building, I've tried to be true to the spirit that they liked in Building 20. I've tried to make an environment that, even though it's new, is true to the spirit of the casualness, nonpreciousness, and flexibility that they liked.

The way it was explained to me, I am building a place where all these heroic people, some of them Nobel Prize winners, would work together. If the building could evoke such a sense of community that it would be likely they'd all run into one another, accidentally even, that synergy would be very productive for their ultimate pedagogical and inventive needs. So that's what we tried to do.

BI: This is the part where you're getting to know the clients and their needs better?

FG: I always try to spend time with clients and find out who they are, what they're about, what they're looking for, and how they're dealing with life. Besides hiring me and paying for the work, the second most important thing clients do is to say something about what they want to pay for, and usually I get excited about trying to realize their dream. They have some kind of a fantasy about what they're doing and why they came to me, and I try to understand that and realize that for them. It's important to me that they get what they want and that they don't just get a dumb building and feel like they've been taken advantage of.

It takes a long time to develop these projects, and I never give up. Early in the process, I never say, "Okay, we've done enough. Stop." When I say "Stop," I've exhausted every possibility in trying to find the margins of leverage where you get the most bang for the buck with the ideas that you're playing with, so clients get their money's worth. It isn't true on the MIT project, because it's a university project, but a real estate development project that takes this kind of time quite often gets paid back with extra rents and higher values for the building than an ordinary building. So there is some method to the madness when somebody commissions one of these things. In the case of MIT, they were looking for a building that would attract faculty and students to their campus and programs, because there's a lot of competition for these science people from Silicon Valley and places like that.

BI: How did you get a sense of what they wanted?

FG: We had meetings to talk about it. I also predicted to them in my interview, before they gave me the job, that they would ultimately ask me for offices that exactly replicate what they have now. I told them the story about when I was working at Yale on their psychiatric clinic, I met with clusters of schizophrenic adolescents they treat to get a feel for how they think. One was a very well-dressed young lady, and I asked her what kind of environment she wanted. Without realizing it, she described in infinite detail the room we were in. She described it as what she thought was the proper environment for a treatment space. I felt like I was in some kind of Kafka novel, but it was very fascinating. I told this story to the MIT guys, and I said, "I predict you guys are going to be like that girl."

They laughed. Then, once we had the job, I met with ten of them as a representative group. But before I did, I had my office make a dossier on each one of them, with photographs of their offices. They didn't know I had them, and as each one described his needs, I was looking at a photo of his office, and it was damn close to what he was describing.

Because they're not into design and architecture, they don't understand the possibilities. They can't speculate or fantasize about what it might be like. They can only think of it as what it is. At the end of the meeting, I told them they did exactly what I predicted. They replied: "Oh God. How do we get out of our rut?"

So I said, "Let's study other cultures as examples," and we made models of other cultures. We asked, What if this cluster of offices was treated like a classic Japanese house, with all the shoji Japanese screens and a big room in the center with all the offices surrounding it? You can close it all off and have separation, or you can open it all up and have everybody together. Then we made a model which was a colonial house with two floors. You would come into a central space with a stairway where you go up to the senior scientists' office at the top. The younger students and staff would be on the bottom, which creates a hierarchy.

I was trying to do what they'd asked me to do, which was to crack them open. We also created a website which the 400 students, 250 faculty, and the administration—about 700 people altogether—could access. I knew it was risky, and in hindsight I think it was *really* risky, but we did it. We would constantly refill the website with pictures of the models, and all kinds of things we were thinking about that related to the project. I said, "We're going to let it all hang out for you, and you guys can respond. Here's my e-mail address." And I got some hateful e-mail for a while.

BI: Do you remember any of it?

FG: Yes. They did research on older projects. You know, everybody has some ghosts, especially when you're a young architect starting out, so they dug deep and found some things that would be problematic for them. I was interested in the extent to which they went to discredit me. Not a lot of people—just a few.

I don't think it was done with hostility. It's the way scientists think. They try to get to the essence of things. They think, This is what you did there, therefore what are you going to do here? Some of it was painful to read, but I think in the end it was worth it because slowly they realized that I was listening to them. They understood that I was being responsive to their needs and trying to make the architecture out of that.

It took about a year or so. But because they were involved and were able to say these things to me, I think they became believers. With the size of the models that we've prepared, they've also been able to see what we're doing that way. We've taken them inside with Web cameras, so they can understand the space. We've made mock-ups of their offices in Cambridge, in a warehouse, so they can go in and sit at desks in offices like they're going to get, and criticize the furniture. They've already done that, and we've made modifications. It's a process I really love. I enjoy the people part of it, probably as much as I do the design.

BI: What were some of the specific concerns on this project?

FG: There were three donors, and originally they wanted the building to have three personas, which I think got us on the track of these figural towers. But when we split it into three personas, the building suggested three different enclaves and there wasn't any interaction, which seemed to represent the opposite of what they were trying to accomplish. So over time we tried to have our cake and eat it, too, where the three parts looked like separate elements yet were a family. That's why they look like a family of vertical shapes. They are almost anthropomorphic. They're robotic in character, which is circumstantial because we couldn't afford a lot of curved material.

BI: It wasn't planned that they were to be robotic?

FG: No. But you can see how you get there. You're trying to make an enclave, and you start out making three separate buildings and joining them. When that doesn't work, you try to mix it up and you almost just naturally go to the cocktail party format, where there are a lot of different people in the same room talking to each other, and that sort of represents what the building stands for. A good friend of mine, the landscape architect Laurie Olin, said it reminded him of the painter Fernand Léger, and once he said it, I couldn't get it out of my head. There is some truth in that, although I wasn't looking at Léger. Nor was I thinking of Léger.

BI: What determined your choice of materials?

FG: The selection of materials is based on the character of the place and the light.

BI: That was so clear when you were designing the Center for the Visual Arts at the University of Toledo in the early 1990s. The copper you chose there looked like pewter once you put a lead coating on it. What prompted that choice?

Gehry found beauty in lead-coated copper, which resembles pewter in the Toledo light, for his Center for the Visual Arts at the Toledo Art Museum.

FG: I loved the lead-coated copper because it looked beautiful with the light. It did look like pewter, and I was fascinated with it. There are many domes made of lead-coated copper at Yale, which I'd seen and liked, and I was into the metal anyway from the beginning. I could do three-dimensional buildings all in one material. You could do roofs and walls, and when I did the Ron Davis house in Los Angeles, I did it all in metal. So I was looking for materials that could do that, and the problem with copper is that it looks black for ten years. I used copper for other projects, but it's not nice for a long time until it turns green. You'd have to pre-green it, and in the old days, they used to pour horse urine all over it so it would be green.

If the building was sheathed in lead copper, it would turn green in fifty years, as the lead washed off the surface of the copper. We used it in Boston on

Gehry design partner Craig Webb notes that the Stata Center's "architectural diversity" of brick, aluminum, and varying window treatments helps break down the project's scale.

the Newbury Street [commercial] project there in the mid-eighties, and then I decided to use it in Toledo. That material's subsequently been declared illegal. Almost all over the world, you can't use it because the lead on the surface does wash off and it goes into the water table. It's a very negligible amount actually, and it's more psychological than real, but it was outlawed. The Toledo Center will ultimately turn green in fifty years, but I probably won't see it. I'd like to come back and see it.

BI: At the Stata Center, a lot of the building is brick.

FG: Yes. We were going to select a color that relates to the Cambridge brick. We're going to use white surfaces in some cases, with the brick, because as you go through Cambridge, there's a kind of tradition of white and brick that's really beautiful. Because I lived there for a while, it's in my consciousness. I'm aware of those things. And the metal we use because it's easy to do shapes in the metal.

BI: You mean the stainless steel?

FG: Any metal surface we use is easy, because I can shape it. It's the cheapest material to shape.

BI: You use titanium in the canopies. Is there a particular reason for that?

FG: Just for the color. We wanted some color, and we liked the titanium colors. So we're using a little bit in there. But as for stainless steel versus titanium, we're using stainless because it's cheaper. I never really entertained doing the whole building in titanium, because I knew we couldn't afford it.

BI: What led to the building that has a spout?

FG: Rod Brooks, who is director of MIT's artificial intelligence lab, is on the building committee. At one of our meetings, he and his group raised the issue, as did some of the others, of whether there was a way that people outside could see what's going on inside the building. Could there be a way of communicating how many people were in the building, at, say, midnight? So we have two fortune-teller crystal balls outside—on a rooftop and above an entryway—which are very expensive pieces, and even more expensive are the electronics inside of them, which will in fact have data and tell people what's going on.

BI: These will be broadcast on the outside using slides and things like that?

FG: Yes, but much more high-tech. It's digital imagery. It'll have form and color. They'll be able to project a picture of someone like Bill Gates.

Then Rod asked for something for his department. He has a robot called Cog that's learning from its mistakes. Cog is getting smarter every day, so the idea is that when Cog comes up with some great breakthrough, a puff of smoke will go up through the chimney. That's kind of a nice, fairly cheap trick.

BI: Were you excited by all this high-tech, advanced research? Is that one of the things that intrigued you about it?

FG: Yes, I got all excited about meeting these bloody geniuses and mixing it up with them. I thought I'd learn something. And I did. A lot of stuff.

BI: What did you learn?

FG: I learned that one of the fastest creatures on earth is the cockroach. And they make robots to simulate that.

BI: Do you think Stata Center really pushes the envelope? Were you trying to make it as technologically advanced a building as you could for people who were so technologically advanced?

Gehry says he was "building a place where all these heroic people, some of them Nobel Prize winners, would work together."

FG: We tried to do that. These are people who invent the greatest control mechanisms for heating, cooling, telephones, lighting, and communications, so we did a lot of research on their work. We were planning things like you could walk into your office and say, "Hi, I'm Rod," and the lights would go on. It's easy to do that now and fairly cheap. You can go into an office and say, "Call Professor Smith," and the telephone will dial Professor Smith's number and then his face will come up on the screen.

We presumed they were going to want all that. Then we had a meeting with the ten professors who represented the project, and we talked to them about all this high-tech stuff. After a while, one of them said, "Look, I really want one of those old-fashioned thermostats, and I really want just a normal light switch. I don't want all that stuff." Then a couple of others said the same thing, and before the meeting was over they all said, "Yes, that's what we want." Although they're inventing all this stuff, they're not so eager to live with it.

In mid-2007, Gehry and I talked again about Stata, which he had recently visited.

BI: Are you happy with the Stata Center?

FG: It always works for me when it works for the client, because that's what I start off to do. But I was disappointed that Noam Chomsky didn't like it, because I love Chomsky. When he was in Building 20, he had a lot of space for his books and papers, and he probably didn't like being squeezed into a little office on the sixth floor. He deserves better.

BI: The Student Street works nicely.

FG: Well, they already have their "endless corridor," which goes throughout the school. I just connected into it and gave them my version of it. That's all. And my version is more user-friendly than theirs. When I was at MIT for something else, I walked through it. There, on a big blackboard, someone had written, "Frank Gehry, we love you." And they didn't know I was coming.

Just a few months later, The Boston Globe *reported that MIT had filed a lawsuit charging that Gehry Partners and Skanska USA Building Inc. were responsible for "design and construction failures" which caused leaks and other problems at Stata Center. As accusations rushed through the media and blogosphere, architecture critics like the* Globe's *Robert Campbell observed that daring architects require daring clients who take into consideration the accompanying risks.*

Gehry's "Student Street" connects with MIT's existing "endless corridor."

Writing about "starchitects" several weeks later, the New York Times *architecture critic Nicolai Ouroussoff added that "as a rule, if a roof leaks in a Frank Gehry building, it's headline news; if the building was designed by a hack commercial architect, the leak is ignored, at least as news."*

BI: What about the leaks you've been charged with at the Stata Center?

FG: Why would you talk about that? Why would you even give it credence?

BI: Well, you've been talking about it everywhere else, so we should talk about it here.

FG: The problem is that at this point I don't know what the indictment is in the MIT lawsuit. We worked with various local contractors and subcontractors on that job. It's probably easily fixed, if it is there, but MIT never said,

"Frank Gehry, the building's leaking. Help us." These things are normally handled by insurance companies.

BI: How did it make its way into the press?

FG: MIT filed a lawsuit, and the filing of a suit is in the public domain. Eager reporters are always there ready to take you out, so there they were. And I feel like the reporters don't do their due diligence. They just shoot from the hip. They don't care. And that happens all the time. It happened at Bilbao. They wrote about it as a "rusting hulk," without realizing that titanium doesn't rust.

With the 2006 release of both the Gehry Collection at Tiffany's and Sydney Pollack's Sketches of Frank Gehry, *entirely new audiences were introduced to designer Gehry. The film has played in movie theaters and on television networks around the world, and Tiffany's has similarly premiered its Gehry Collection in more and more stores.*

Gehry has been designing furniture and other products, often very successfully, nearly as long as he has been designing buildings. But little could compare with the brouhaha surrounding his Tiffany line. Inaugurated and maintained with huge ad campaigns—and, of course, the sheer beauty of what's being sold—the Tiffany venture has made Gehry a consumer icon much as Guggenheim Museum Bilbao made him an architectural one.

How does inspiration translate to products as well as buildings? His design philosophy: "Creative people are always trying to do something new. It's in their DNA to not want to do what the other guy did."

BI: You've explored so many product lines over the years—chairs, lamps, watches.

FG: Architects have done things like this all their lives. Sometimes, as in the case of the cardboard furniture—and this happens to me all the time—I come up with an idea and I test it very quickly. Then I don't continue because in my mind I've figured it all out, so it's not interesting to go ahead. But then I started making the old cardboard furniture new again, because I had a lot of ideas back then that I never explored. When I had someone working here who liked to do that kind of work, I thought I'd play with him and see what we could do, so we started making a bunch of new old pieces.

There are new lamps, too. We developed the technology and how to make and produce them, which is what I did with the cardboard furniture. I love to do that. I love the technology of it.

BI: You seem to love both, the technology and the application of the technology.

FG: I do, but I also like to subvert the technology so that the technology isn't driving it and so that there's a casual anti-technology. The technology of it is impeccable, but I made it look like it isn't.

BI: Is it a problem reconciling the differences between product design and architecture?

FG: Well, it doesn't always work. On some earlier products I tried, there was a big difference between our design process and their way of doing things. We do study models, and by the time we do a study model, they're fabricating. They just go right into it. They can't change it, and you sometimes get caught. I don't know how to talk to them.

As I said, I have a way of opening my own doors to new things and playing with them and getting excited about them and then not following through. Because I'll play out all the permutations and combinations in my head, I lose interest, and so I've got to have something new. What sometimes happens is that I go back to it, and I've kept coming back to product design. I designed a toaster, picture frames, glassware, a vodka bottle. We spent a huge amount of office time on these products before I closed that down.

BI: Let's go back to the cardboard furniture in the 1960s and early 1970s.

FG: I was doing the Joseph Magnin store in Costa Mesa. The problem as it was stated to me was that fashions were changing so quickly that the fixturing became obsolete. So they asked me to see if there was some less expensive way to make fixtures that could be thrown away, and naturally I went to cardboard.

Saying, "Cardboard is essentially this," Gehry picks up some paper, fiddles with it, and shows me how it can be folded to become structural.

Gehry's design for the Wyborowa vodka bottle recalls the torque of his earlier Ustra office building in Hanover, Germany.

FG: That's what paper does, and cardboard is a variation of that. Most people would say that if you're going to use a material like cardboard for furniture, you would just fold it a couple of times, make structural shapes, and it would be very efficient. But I didn't like how it looked.

BI: So how did you get to the next step, where you liked the way it looked?

FG: We used contoured layers of cardboard as terrain for our site models, and one day I was sitting in my office looking at the exposed end of it. I thought, That's beautiful. Why don't I just use that? So I started to make shapes with it, which were very fuzzy, with a nice texture. I loved it, because it was like corduroy. You get a texture that's pleasant, and I could make a table-top that wasn't very heavy, which seemed promising. It trumps folding the

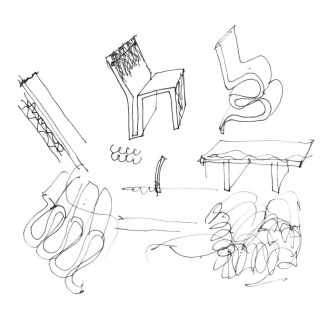

The quickly made Easy Edges cardboard chairs, designed between 1969 and 1973, were exciting for Gehry because intuition and product were so directly linked.

cardboard, and very efficiently you get a structure that's very strong and aesthetically looks great.

With such creative partners as Robert Irwin, Jack Brogan, and Greg Walsh, Gehry in 1969 came up with his first line of furniture, Easy Edges, using corrugated cardboard to create chairs, desks, and tables. It was too late to incorporate the notion for the Magnin stores, but the furniture soon had a life of its own, evolving into a collection sold in department stores. It was a critical success, but it became too much of a distraction for Gehry. He lost money, time, and maybe a few friends, he says, and it would be a while before he went back to furniture design.

BI: It didn't work out, but you've spoken of the cardboard furniture as one of the most exciting things you'd ever worked on. Why?

FG: Well it was exciting because it was more instant. It was that direct link between intuition and product. It was closer to making art because I would do a sketch for a chair in the morning and Jack Brogan would make the chair by afternoon. If I was going to somebody's house for dinner that night, I'd take it and give it to them instead of a bottle of wine. I gave most of them away.

Gehry starts naming people he gave the chairs to, then sighs audibly.

BI: Your Experimental Edges in the late 1970s and early 1980s were again corrugated and laminated cardboard, and then there was that whole series of bentwood furniture for Knoll International in the 1990s. Wasn't the Knoll line inspired in part by bushel baskets you played with as a child?

FG: Yes. When I was a kid I used to see fruit delivered to the house in bushel baskets. I would sit on the baskets, which were bouncy,

Gehry says bouncy bushel baskets used to deliver fruit when he was a child were the genesis of his furniture designs for Knoll.

and when I started doing furniture, I remembered that and tried to emulate the bounciness. I made a bunch of bouncy pillows out of wood, and they worked. I was really excited, and I made a chair or two out of it, and they worked. By the time you got through all the tests that you had to make, you couldn't keep it that thin and bounce. But it was the genesis of the furniture I've done with Knoll.

BI: You always seem to have something going on that doesn't have to do with architecture.

FG: Let me tell you them as they come into my head. There's the cardboard furniture, the new one-of-a-kind pieces, which were made in limited editions. We developed paper lighting for Vitra, and the Cloud Lamps were made for Vitra by the Belux company. I'm doing the plastic furniture with Heller, and aluminum furniture with Emeco. It's commerce for them. For me it's an invention process, and there's a bit of a conflict. When Tiffany came in, I was a lot smarter about it.

Gehry's Cloud Lamps are among several products he has designed in recent years.

BI: How did the Tiffany designs come about?

FG: The Tiffany line came about indirectly. I had two or three encounters about jewelry that were sort of crazy. One night I was at a dinner, sitting between two very wealthy ladies, and I didn't have anything much to talk about, so I made up something. I said, "You know, I have this idea that I want to take the floor plan of Bilbao, make it the size of a brooch, and fill it with diamonds." They both looked at me and said, "That sounds great. How much do you think something like that would cost?" When I said it would be a million dollars at least, the first woman said, "God, I'd love to have one," and the other lady said, "I'd like to have one, too. And I know five other people who would also love it."

I forgot about the conversation until maybe two years later, when I was at a fund-raiser and again sitting between two wealthy ladies. When the lady on my right said she was in the diamond business, it triggered the memory and I told her about my idea.

BI: The Bilbao-on-a-brooch idea?

FG: Well, Bilbao, and by then I'd added more buildings—Disney Hall and a few others. She told me she'd

Tiffany's diamond Bilbao Brooch, set in platinum, is signed by Frank Gehry and sells for $1,000,000.

love to work on it with me and that she had gorgeous diamonds. When I cautioned her that they would cost a million dollars or more, she said, "It doesn't matter. There are plenty of customers." That apparently included the lady on my left, who, listening to this, said she'd buy one. I don't know if they were serious, but I think they were. So when Disney Hall was trying to raise another five million dollars, I suggested we call Tiffany and try making some brooches and selling them.

Tiffany wasn't interested in that idea, but they were interested in me. Later, they selected nine designers, and we arranged to have two days of meetings every six weeks. We alternated between LA and New York.

BI: What would you do in those meetings?

FG: I would sketch things, or I would take the designers around my office and out into the studio to find things that interested us. We'd scavenge around looking for things to pirate. Remember that when we started, it was more about Tiffany vases, dishes, candlesticks, and things like that. I didn't expect to be doing jewelry at first.

BI: Give me a sense of process. So they walk in . . .

FG: With a bunch of wax. I'd sketch out some designs on paper or on the computer. They would go back and make their own drawings and waxes, and both the drawings and waxes originally turned me off. So it got hairy for a while. I didn't know how to talk to them.

Tiffany's "Rough Diamond and Keshi Pearl" mesh necklace in 18-karat white gold is signed by Gehry and sells for $750,000. Photo: Richard Pierce

Then they actually made some of the jewelry. I realized they knew what they were doing and they knew how to translate my ideas. So I trusted them more, and we began to free-associate and make new things. At one point, I went on the computer and took a building shape that we'd been working on, and because of the software we had, we could stretch, extrude, pull, and twist the shape. That's how I made the shape they call "orchid."

BI: It's the same notion, isn't it, of using technology to take you further with whatever the idea is?

FG: Right. But that's just one method. Look at the mesh in these necklaces.

Gehry holds up a sterling silver mesh necklace dotted with diamonds and pearls. By the look on his face, he clearly adores it.

FG: They brought it in and asked what I thought. I love that mesh, so I started fooling with it. They had been bringing me goodies, and I had a little can of uncut diamonds, which I think were from their diamond mine, and I just grabbed a handful of the diamonds and threw it on the mesh. Then they added pearls.

BI: That was the necklace Anjelica Huston was wearing when they launched the Gehry Collection in Beverly Hills, isn't it?

Gehry smiles. Huston was the last part of the equation.

FG: I was in New York when Tiffany's opened the line there, and there was a gorgeous young actress looking at the jewelry. Since it was all lying around on the counters and I could do whatever I wanted, I picked the necklace up and put it on her. She was wearing a green bare-back dress, so I just flipped it over her neck so it was lying across her back, and God, it was just so incredible.

It became obvious to me that it was like a building—you design it, people work on it, it gets built, it's finished, there's the opening, and then what happens? It all comes to life with people in it. The same thing happens with jewelry when you put it on—it comes to life, as it were.

BI: So you're having fun with this.

FG: I am. I want to do more. I did some candlesticks. They look like melted wax. They're really gorgeous.

So is a white Tiffany vase on the shelf just beyond his worktable. Where did that idea come from? I ask him.

Gehry also designed Tiffany's Rock vase in bone china.

FG: I was at the artist Tony Berlant's for dinner one night, maybe two years ago. He was showing me his prehistoric rock collection, and I went gaga over those rocks. So he said, "Why don't you take a few and just look at them for a while. You'll probably get an idea." I took them with me, and I kept looking at them. If you look at the model of my new house, it looks like the prehistoric rocks gone crazy. I don't know where I'm going with it, but I'm playing with it right now.

BI: In other words, everything is inspiration?

FG: It is. When I was starting out, I used to go around to the industrial section of Los Angeles and take photographs. I don't think those buildings are there anymore, but they had a quality to them like the film *Metropolis*. You could look at them and fantasize. I was interested in the buildings that were least important in the world, that had some weird intrinsic beauty. You didn't have to spend so much money to create architecture with industrial materials.

I'm very opportunistic. I think of it like the cat with the ball of twine. You've got your ball of twine, you push it, and it falls somewhere. You pounce on it and take advantage of it. I think that's what art is about, that exploring. People have written tons of essays about the psyche and how art manifests itself. But it's basically a person's response to an environment and a given set of conditions. Sometimes it's done with painting, sometimes with clay, and architects do it through a construction process. There is, in the preparing, a sense of accident. But it isn't just accident, because accident implies it is uninformed. You study art history and architectural history, and you come to the fray with a certain learning and understanding. It's an informed accident. Does that make sense?

BI: There's a Zen saying that when the student is ready, the teacher appears. That's what you're talking about, isn't it?

FG: Look at the Tiffany vase and then the curvy bronze thing to the right of it. I've been looking at them for the last few weeks, at different times. I want to do a building that looks like those two things. When you look at them together, you can see there's a nice urban composition there.

BI: Like Fred and Ginger?

FG: Yes, like Fred and Ginger. I think it's all similar, and that's why it's possible to play in all these arenas. I think it's fine for an architect to design jewelry.

BI: What about an architect starring in a film? How did your friend Sydney Pollack come to make *Sketches of Frank Gehry*?

FG: I got a lot of requests from different places to do a documentary. I guess Bilbao sparked it, and there was interest from the BBC, Canadian CBC, PBS, a couple of others.

BI: Why did you choose Pollack?

FG: Sydney was invited to the opening of Bilbao in 1997 as a friend of the family. I never expected him to be there. I was in the atrium being interviewed,

Gehry photographed old industrial buildings in Los Angeles that he thought had "some weird intrinsic beauty."

Sydney Pollack's 1997 snapshots of the Guggenheim Bilbao were Gehry's favorite photographs of the new museum.

GUGGENHEIM MUSEUM BILBAO, 1997. PHOTO: © SYDNEY POLLACK

and I saw someone looking in the window. He started waving at me, and when I realized it was Sydney, I excused myself from the interview and ran over to open the door. They wouldn't let him in, so he had been walking around the building with his little camera, taking pictures. He told me that the building knocked him out. He had never seen anything like it. He went on and on. So I finished my interview, and I took him on a tour of the building. I think he stayed that night for the festivities, and then a few weeks later he sent me the pictures.

When all those people wanted to do documentaries, a friend asked me who took the best pictures of my buildings. I said a lot of different people took pictures, but the best photographs ever of Bilbao were done by Sydney. That's all I said, and then a few weeks later she called and invited me to dinner. I went, and there was Sydney. It was just the three of us, and she starts pitching him on the documentary. I was kind of embarrassed about it all.

BI: You mean you wouldn't have asked him yourself?

FG: I thought he'd be busy with all kinds of Hollywood stuff and wouldn't want to do this. But to my surprise, he called a few weeks later and said okay. He hired filmmaker Ultan Guilfoyle, who had worked at the Guggenheim and who I knew, put together a team, and started following me around. It didn't take that much of my time, because they spent more time with other people and with the buildings.

GUGGENHEIM MUSEUM BILBAO, 1997. PHOTO: © SYDNEY POLLACK

BI: When did Pollack decide to actually be in the film?

FG: One day Sydney had a camera on his shoulder when Ultan was filming both of us. Sydney said he didn't know if it would work, but he felt if he brought in a full camera crew, it wouldn't be as easy for us to talk on camera. He asked me, "Do you mind if I try this? Ultan is going to just record it, so I can get a sense of it." That worked so well the few times he did it that I said to him, "You know, I think you should do more of this with me, because it feels right."

BI: How did you feel when you saw the film?

FG: Sydney was worried about that, so he had Berta and me over to his house for dinner and ran the film for us. He said, "If you want to change anything, now is the time. Tell me. But this is where I'm going with it." I liked it, and I think I felt more comfortable than if it had been shot without him being in it. Having somebody in it with me took some of the heat off.

He took me to Toronto for the first screening, which was at the Toronto International Film Festival. I sat beside him in a six-hundred-seat theater, an architecture critic on my left and Sydney on my right. I had to sit through the whole screening, wondering what was going to happen when it ended and waiting to see how people would react to it.

Sydney Pollack photographs
the new museum.

Pollack and Gehry at
Guggenheim Bilbao

BI: It's a lot different premiering a building, isn't it?

FG: Buildings are slower as they enter the world. You have a lot of preparation time. By the time it opens to the public, everybody's seen it, there's been talk, articles have been published about it, and the actual opening is anticlimactic. But this was excruciating. All I could think of, sitting there, was, What if they didn't stand up and clap? What if they just get up and leave? Boy, I never want to go through that again. Afterwards, Sydney and I went out and just drank ourselves into oblivion.

DUAL COASTS: ATLANTIC YARDS AND GRAND AVENUE

A *few years into the twenty-first century, much of Gehry's time and staff focused on massive redevelopment work for Los Angeles's Grand Avenue and Brooklyn's Atlantic Yards. Both projects required considerable government oversight, experienced construction delays, and received continuing press coverage and, particularly in Brooklyn, scrutiny from neighborhood residents, bloggers, and others.*

Los Angeles's $3 billion, nine-acre Grand Avenue development, called "The Grand," hopes to revitalize that city's downtown cultural and civic core with assorted Gehry-designed properties adjacent to his famed Walt Disney Concert Hall. The first phase of the three-phase project includes two high-rise residential towers, one of them housing a 275-room Mandarin Oriental Hotel.

Ironically, Grand Avenue's developer, Related Companies, announced a $100 million infusion of equity from investors in Dubai the very same week in March 2008 that developer Forest City Ratner Companies acknowledged possible postponement of parts of the Brooklyn project. The $4 billion, twenty-two-acre Atlantic Yards project was originally intended to include a basketball arena, housing, offices, and retail space, but developer Bruce Ratner told The New York Times *that the country's troubled economy might delay things. While the 18,000-seat arena for the New Jersey Nets—destined to be renamed the Brooklyn Nets—remained on schedule, Ratner conceded that other construction might be postponed.*

At the time of this conversation in August 2005, however, Gehry was just beginning work on both projects, and he was clearly excited about the chance to do all that urban design.

FG: As I said earlier, when I went to school and studied planning, my fantasy was urban design. What happens now is that buildings are built haphazardly, one or two at a time, and there's no real sense of community. They're just economic engines that somebody puts together, usually not with architects who think about things other than doing what the client needs. It's rare for an architect to get a piece of a city and have the chance to build at that great an urban scale.

BI: Which leads us, of course, to the Atlantic Yards project you're designing in Brooklyn for Bruce Ratner.

FG: Bruce and I met on the New York Times building competition several years ago, and we got along really well. He called me later and said he had been thinking of me since then and wanted to work with me. He said he loved our proposal for the New York Times building and was sorry we withdrew, and he was now doing a project that entailed planning a large neighborhood. It was about six or seven million square feet, including an arena, housing, and commercial space, and it was the kind of thing I've been waiting all my life to get to do.

I worked on such things when I was working for Victor Gruen, in the 1950s, but other people made the design decisions. I was just a project manager, with very little design input, but I saw the developer mentality in doing housing and shopping centers and commercial buildings. I had experience observing how they think and what their priorities are. I watched them process ideas and learned how things went together. I was ready if something came along.

BI: But then you waited, what, fifty years?

FG: Not really. I did Santa Monica Place in 1978 for the Rouse Company, and we designed it as a mixed-use project, not just as a dumb shopping center. Then, for reasons beyond my control, the city wouldn't support it, and so it ended up being just a shopping center. But even with that, I tried to break it down in scale so it wasn't a monolithic building. The mall itself I opened at both ends so it became like a street. It didn't terminate with the department stores.

BI: There was also the smaller Edgemar urban design project in Santa Monica a few years later.

FG: At Edgemar, the client, Abby Sher, was willing to risk flying in the face of traditional leasing programs to try and develop a really beautiful public space that would be inhabited by and would relate to restaurants, small shops, art and offices, so it's a mixed-use project. It was very hands-on for her, and she made it work. She willed it into existence.

There's something else about Edgemar. It's very hard to create a public space, and this was set back from the street. It was important to create an interior square that you could visualize from outside and which would invite you in. That's why the entries are on the diagonal, so as you walk by on the street you can see in.

BI: Were there other instances of urban planning over the years?

FG: I did master planning studies in the late 1960s for the city of Hermosa Beach, California, including low-income housing, which wasn't realized. There was middle-class housing at Bixby Green in Garden Grove in 1968, and then something for the Irvine Company called University Park in 1970. Those are fairly big projects.

I was always taking on things like that whenever I could. A few years ago I did a low-income housing project, about three hundred houses, called Goldstein, in Frankfurt, and we did some planning studies for the Frankfurt city government for other projects that weren't realized. Goldstein came out very successfully, and I go back to see it. It's still functioning very well.

BI: I didn't know about all these projects, and I'm assuming the general public doesn't know about them either.

FG: Stuff doesn't just fall out of a tree, you know. People think that I've never done anything like it, but I also did a high-rise housing tower for Rouse years ago, in Baltimore. So I've done all the parts, let's say.

BI: Did Ratner know all this?

FG: Yes. Bruce had done his homework. He said he had studied my work and realized I was an urban planner but hadn't had the chance to do that.

I also liked the project because it was Brooklyn. I actually lived there

The Edgemar development in Santa Monica, California, uses a diagonal entry to invite passersby into its public spaces.

when I was a year old, on Avenue J in Flatbush, but I don't remember much. And my kids moved there. My daughter Brina is moving back to Manhattan, but Leslie bought an apartment there. My son Alejo moved back there.

Politically it also appealed to me. The idea of bringing a sports team back to Brooklyn is very powerful, because they lost one. It's been like a big hole in their gut since they lost the Dodgers, and I think Bruce is doing it for the same reason. He loves that idea. And we have to do it right. Bruce said he didn't want to just do an arena that looks like all the others. He wanted it to have the intimacy and relationship between the players and spectators that Disney Hall has between the orchestra and the audience. He told his partners they had to see Disney Hall, and he brought them all out here to do that.

BI: Had you ever thought about doing an arena before?

FG: Well, I go to hockey games a lot, and I can't help but analyze what's wrong with the arenas I've gone to. Staples Center is a complete disaster when

Gehry designed the low-income housing project called Goldstein in Frankfurt, Germany, in 1996.

it comes to what we're talking about. It's purely a money machine. Somebody said, "We don't need any fancy architects telling us what to do." I don't go, a lot of my friends don't go, and some of the people who don't go are really important hockey fans. It's not a user-friendly place, but, ironically, it's the most profitable arena in the country. The reason is they've got two basketball teams, the Lakers and the Clippers, and they've got the LA Kings, and it's a big venue for concerts and other events. LA has needed a place like that.

BI: How are things progressing?

FG: We've developed the plans for the Brooklyn arena now, which are very tight and very much a new spirit for the inside. We're also working on solving the incredibly complicated issues of the traffic in and out of the arena at peak hours. It's very complicated. It's very exciting.

BI: What about the rest of the Atlantic Yards project? All those structures besides the arena?

The planned arena for Atlantic Yards in Brooklyn will showcase the New Jersey Nets, which would be renamed the Brooklyn Nets.

FG: Bruce Ratner emotionally and intellectually understands that when you go to the next step architecturally, it will pay off. He's worked with many good architects in attempts to raise the bar for developers, but his parent company's architectural DNA is a little dicey. I kid him and say, "The DNA is going to be counter to it."

Sometimes it is, and that's when I call him and say, "Your DNA is showing." And the reason to work with him over others is that I can talk to him like that. Implicit is the understanding of a partnership to do something excellent, knowing full well that on the way there are factors and economic issues that are milestones that he has to meet, and I have to understand and realize they're not arbitrary. I can't just say, "Oh, damn developers doing blah, blah, blah . . ." I can't do that with this guy because he's committed to doing something excellent. And he equally has to understand that there are aspirations in architecture that have to be fulfilled for me to be happy and for us to be mutually happy.

We're working with New York's Department of City Planning and its director, Amanda Burden. So far there's a lot of agreement about general urban goals, and we mostly see eye-to-eye. We've gotten a lot of support from Mayor [Michael] Bloomberg. And Ratner and his team work really well with my team. They like each other, and they even spend social time together. They sometimes have to travel together, so everybody has kind of bonded, me included. For what I've yearned to do, it's kind of the dream project.

Maybe my romantic notion of democracy is that you break down the scale of the city and differentiate it so there's not an overpowering Albert Speer kind of architectural statement. That's what I'm trying to do, and Bruce Ratner is absolutely committed to this on every level. He understands what I'm trying to do. And it's really hard to do.

BI: There are so many pieces.

FG: One part develops and then it eclipses the others, so you have to go back and do the other over again.

BI: There's also the notion that you're designing this entire project yourself. That's a huge undertaking.

FG: Normally on a project like this, since there are twelve buildings, you say, "Well, maybe I shouldn't do them all. Maybe we should bring in two or three other architects," because that's the way a city would be built. But Bruce knew that I was prone to do that, so he said from the beginning, "One of the conditions of you getting this project is that you do it all yourself. I don't want to deal with a lot of people. It will go faster if I can just work with one office."

BI: What did you think when he said that?

FG: Well, it upped the ante. I'm playing against myself, building to building. And I'm trying to take a pluralistic approach to it, so it's not a unified building model and doesn't look like one overpowering idea. I want it to fit better into the context of Brooklyn.

Sketch and model (opposite page) from Atlantic Yards development set for Brooklyn

It also made the challenge more exciting in a way because I had to figure out a design strategy. With one architect doing something that big, it could end up looking like a project. I wouldn't like it. Other people wouldn't like it. So to compose this with lots of variety, so it didn't feel like a project, is one of the keys. It's hard to disguise your hand, and you can't exactly do it, but we're using a very simple blocky kind of architecture for most of it, so it's generic.

BI: Blocky?

FG: It's like blocks. It doesn't have a lot of curves. That allows it to be more traditional, and the subtleties and proportioning of the windows and setbacks and such humanize it. Within that, we're developing a variety of window systems. I look at it like composing a Brandenburg concerto, which has a coda but layering. It builds up notes as it goes, and then it shifts into another octave. It adds different instruments and changes the character as it unfolds. And it's very rich. The Brandenburg concertos are among the richest pieces of music I've ever heard.

I think of this development as having that kind of possibility. The buildings are now getting pretty set in shapes, and we're starting to work on the windows. Those are things you do that don't have big cost implications. The sub-

tlety of windows, the changes, aren't that complicated, nor are they expensive, but the variety creates a richness. So the whole game with this project has been to keep layering richness on as it gets to each stage of definition and to build in veins of visual richness that continue. It's frustrating, and it's very slow. It's like watching paint dry, but at the end of a few months, it's very intense. You can feel it when you look at the models now.

BI: Is it difficult to explain all this to clients who may not be inclined to essentially watch paint dry?

FG: It's frustrating when you try to explain that process to a new client in advance. The norm in architectural circles for these people has been that the architect does a scheme very quickly, then builds it. They're not used to the six-month period that I take to slog through this. But at the end of that period, when you do it this way, the work is bulletproof almost. Everything is so essen-

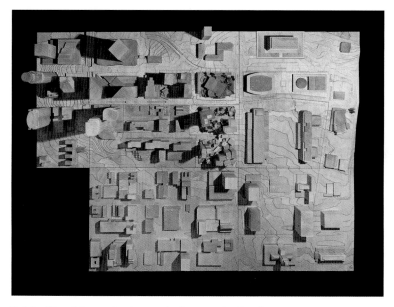

Models of Grand Avenue development in downtown Los Angeles

tial that you can't take anything out without upsetting the house of cards, and that's fascinating to me. You have to be thinking budget control all the way through, because at the end, it's always more money. Part of that six-month design process is also concurrently honing in on the budget, so that it's build-able within the constraints of the client's pocketbook.

BI: Are you talking generally or are you talking specifically about this project?

FG: Generally. But it applies here. It's the hardest thing for a new client to understand who hasn't experienced it with me.

BI: Is it still hard for new clients to understand once they've seen how you work?

FG: Bruce understands it now, but the new Grand Avenue clients—this is going to be a learning curve for them.

BI: Let's talk about Grand Avenue. I know this isn't the first time you've been involved in attempts to develop downtown and particularly Grand Avenue.

FG: Before Disney Hall, I worked on a team for Grand Avenue, led by the developer Rob Maguire, that was competing with other developers to build a Grand Avenue that would link together all of downtown's cultural facilities. It would become a quasi-pedestrian street, conducive to parades and street dances, and the dream of that competition certainly never left me and never left Maguire and never left a lot of people in the city. We had all these ideas about how to make Grand Avenue more livable and usable, but that plan went nowhere. Disney Hall was going to be the first new piece since the Museum of Contemporary Art opened in the eighties, and my hope was that this would be a continuation of our Grand Avenue dream.

As part of Disney Hall I did work on Grand Avenue. Again we came up with ways to build European-style plazas, green spaces—a real cultural district. But there was no money to do it. We were told, "Thanks for the effort."

BI: This is a real issue as an architect, isn't it? You spend all that creative time, you have all those hopes and dreams, and then they say, "Thank you. Bye-bye."

FG: Yes, and you don't get paid for it. This is volunteer work for the city. This was trying to be a good citizen and trying to help the community.

BI: Which brings us to the current Grand Avenue project.

FG: There are three parcels, one directly across the street from Disney Hall. One is an additional block to the east of Disney and one to the south of Disney, which would be across the street from MOCA. A lot of developers put in to do it, and I was invited to be on the Related team, the guys who did AOL/Time Warner in New York. It was being run by David Childs at Skidmore Owings & Merrill and they needed a local guy, so David asked me to be on it. I decided not to do that. I had another offer from Richard Weintraub, a young developer, who wanted to go for it. We had very frank and open talks about how he probably wouldn't have a chance, but it could begin to give him a profile in the community, and if he put together a brilliant scheme, he could maybe affect the outcome of the project, even though he wouldn't get to do it. I recommended that we bring in an all-star team, and so I got people like [the architects] Harry Cobb, Zaha Hadid, Greg Lynn, Kevin Daly, and the landscape architect Laurie Olin.

Although we had all this design power, it was a developer competition. They wanted to pick a developer first, but they wanted to see the character of the work the developer might do. We spent time putting together a very rough idea of how to approach this, and it's very close to what they're doing actually, but we didn't win.

BI: How did you feel?

FG: I didn't expect to win. I thought we'd get a hearing and we did. We thought our plan was on the side of the angels. It made sense for LA, and after Related won, Eli Broad called and said he wanted me to work with them. I didn't agree to that, but I did agree to help them with the master planning.

When I accepted the master plan job, they said they would give me one of the major buildings to do, and I didn't know whether I wanted it. You know, it's hard to work with developers. You have to question things to move them to another place, and they don't really like to do that. So when they started asking me to do the building, I really didn't want to do it. I tried to push them away, and then they kept coming back, and finally they accepted all my conditions and gave me the whole first parcel to do. They have agreed to doing it using my process, so it's going to be slow but sure. I have no idea how successful we'll be. I'm optimistic. They're coming at it the right way with me.

BI: Wait a minute. After all the public disagreements between you and Eli Broad over your building his house, then about Disney Hall, wasn't it a bit of a surprise to have him on the phone saying, "Hey, Frank, come on over here and get involved in this"?

FG: No, it wasn't a surprise, because Eli and I had made our peace just before the opening of Disney Hall. My wife, who is smarter than I am about things like this, said, "You know, you can go through the rest of your life in LA with this guy, hating each other. But you travel a lot in similar circles so you run into each other, and it's just uncomfortable. You don't really hate him, and he doesn't really hate you. Why don't we have a dinner for him and his wife and thank him for the work he did on Disney Hall. It was an immense effort he put together. He put it back on track and got it built."

So we decided to have a dinner on the stage of the concert hall, three or four weeks before it opened. The interior was pretty much done. The hall was beautiful and pristine and the organ was finished. We had seventy people at tables on the stage. It was 90 percent his guest list. The mayor was there. The publisher of the *Los Angeles Times.* The county supervisors. Some of the city council members. Big law firms that worked with Eli. I invited the Philharmonic music director, Esa-Pekka Salonen, and a few artists who I knew he liked. Concertmaster Martin Chalifour agreed to play unaccompanied Bach. Organist Manuel Rosales agreed to blast a few notes for us, which would be the first time anybody would hear the organ. It was a wonderful event.

BI: This was a major moment for you both, given your history. Were there speeches?

FG: At the appropriate time, I clink-clinked my glass and stood up. I said, "You all know that Eli and I have been battling for a long time, and it's been all over the press. My assessment of it is we're two control freaks and our control mechanisms got tangled up with each other. Berta and I wanted to have this dinner to thank Eli and Edye for their wonderful work on behalf of Walt Dis-

The initial phase of the Grand Avenue project includes residential and hotel towers.

ney Concert Hall and to forget all the past anger and focus on the wonderful project we've made together.

BI: And Broad's reaction?

FG: Eli got up and he said, "Yes, it's true, we've had our differences, but in the end Frank was right. And thank God we followed him." Then Esa-Pekka spoke for the Philharmonic and thanked him. The musicians played, and it was beautiful. Eli was happy. Edye was happy. Everybody left very happy. We got tons of respect from all those fancy people, the very ones who thought I was some kind of a madman.

BI: And Grand Avenue?

FG: The Broads invited us for dinner several weeks later, and we talked about Grand Avenue. He wanted me to be involved, and I think he was sorry that I was on the Weintraub team. He was pretty sure that Related was going to get it. The other team that was competing was Bruce Ratner's company, Forest City, who are my clients in Brooklyn, but by the time they asked me I was already on Weintraub's team, and when Weintraub got kicked out, it was down to Forest City and Related. Forest City asked me if I would be on their team as well, and I was sort of obligated to them because of the project in New York.

BI: So you were pretty much a given.

FG: Friends like Richard Weinstein at UCLA said to me that for the good of the city I had to do it. Richard even said it was my obligation. Everybody was on me, because they knew it was in the realm of possibility. They urged me not to be so reluctant, because they said this is an important project for LA and if it could be done right—and they said I could do it right—it would be a major coup for the city.

You know, I'm always insecure. At the front end, I'm never sure I can do anything. I really do think, What are they talking about? A lot of people could do this. But I was also skeptical about working with those developers. I thought with Forest City I had a chance because I knew them, but with Related, I didn't think they would be willing to go along with me. That changed when Related's Steve Ross and his people came to my office for the first time. They realized I was doing projects like that in Brooklyn. They saw our process and the computer stuff and they realized we were very well organized. It wasn't a flaky thing.

BI: People don't still think you're flaky, do they?

FG: That's going away, but Related is from New York. They didn't know. But coming to my office changed it. Ross had an epiphany, and I know about it because his local representative called me and said, "Boy, you made such an impression on this guy. You've got to do this project." And I said, "No, I'm not going to do it. It's great that he loves me, but so far he hasn't demonstrated that he can handle it." Anyway, we got through all that.

BI: And if you hadn't gotten through all that, would you have walked away?

FG: I told them that if they didn't want to sign the contract, fine, and I meant it. You can't do that unless you mean it, and I'm in the position to mean it. I know that if I take a project on other terms, for me it'll fail. It will be a fight all the way through. I said that to you earlier. I'm ready to walk away at any point that they're not going to have respect for the way I do things.

New York was long the rare major U.S. metropolis with no Gehry buildings, a situation which has been changing in recent years. Prior to the high-profile Atlantic Yards project in Brooklyn, Gehry and architect Gordon Kipping designed a Tribeca store for fashion designer Issey Miyake in 2001. The Richard B. Fisher Center for the Performing Arts at Bard College, some ninety miles north of Manhattan, opened in 2003, a few months before Disney Hall, and, before that, Gehry completed a cafeteria for the Condé Nast headquarters at 4 Times Square.

Curved glass and titanium are used in the cafeteria in Condé Nast's headquarters at 4 Times Square in New York.

PHOTO: ROGER DONG

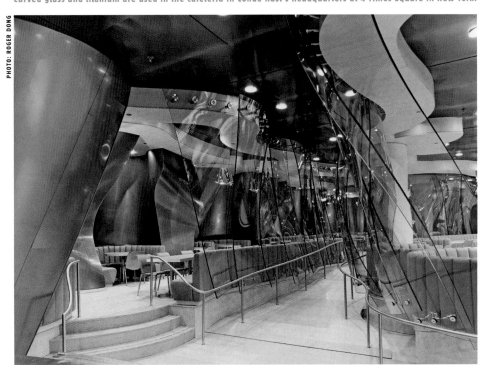

The Condé Nast cafeteria, surrounding diners in curved glass and blue titanium panels, is seen only by people who work in or visit Condé Nast headquarters, however, and Gehry's design partner Edwin Chan has remarked on how nice it would be to build an actual building in glass. When IAC/Interactive Corporation chair Barry Diller decided to build a new headquarters in Chelsea a few years later, Gehry got that chance.

Diller says Gehry was "the only architect who interested me. He and I took a drive in Los Angeles to see Disney Hall, talked about how much we liked sailing, how I liked water, and why we bought this land [by the Hudson River]. Frank did a little sketch, and essentially that's our building. He's a great collaborator. Unlike many other people, he wants to draw in the building owner. He thinks you can't make the building better unless the owner jumps in with both feet."

BI: How did that new headquarters for IAC come about? Did you know Barry Diller from Los Angeles?

FG: I was in Bilbao for the opening there of "The Art of the Motorcycle" [the exhibition on motorcycle design and technology that Gehry designed for the

Gehry's sketch for the IAC building in New York

Guggenheim], and Tom Krens had a reunion there with his motorcycle buddies. When I got there late one morning, they were taking off to go to lunch somewhere, and all these guys were on motorcycles with helmets. I didn't know who they were.

Tom gave me a helmet, indicated a motorcycle, and said, "Get on the back of that one." So I did. We rode for ten or fifteen minutes, and this guy was good. I wasn't scared. When we got to the restaurant, he took off his helmet, and it was Jeremy Irons. A nice guy. He loves architecture, knew who I was, and was very interested. [Former *Los Angeles Times* publisher] Otis Chandler was riding a bike with his wife, Bettina. Barry Diller was with his wife, Diane von Furstenberg. They asked me if I would mind giving them a tour of the Guggenheim. I gave them a tour, and we all sort of bonded. We were all hanging out together.

BI: This was the first time you met Diller?

FG: Yes. I knew Diane from before, because she was on the board of the American Center in Paris, which I'd designed. I had been to some of the board meetings and I had met her there.

BI: So the building came about through this meeting with Diller?

FG: I don't know. I was working on the proposed redevelopment of Lincoln Center [in New York] with Marshall Rose several years ago, and Marshall called me after that. Marshall and I had become friends, and I had known his wife, Candy Bergen, for many years. So one day he called and told me he had a site on the west side where he was doing something with Barry Diller.

BI: This is before or after you met Diller?

FG: I'm sure it was after. Marshall said they were doing this project and were looking for an architect. He also said he didn't think it was something for me. They were really looking for the new Frank Gehry, and did I have any recommendations? It all fit because I knew movie studio people liked Richard Meier and Charles Gwathmey, and I didn't obsess about it. So I recommended Gordon Kipping, a young black architect I know, and a few others. Gordon is very talented, and I knew him well enough to know that he delivers.

BI: Then Rose went away?

FG: He took some names, and I forgot about it. Then I ran into Gordon one day and asked if they'd called, and he said they hadn't. So again I just forgot about it, until one day Marshall called me and said Barry asked why they should get the new Frank Gehry when they could get the real one. And Marshall said it might be good for my career to do this office building in Manhattan.

BI: How did he characterize it?

FG: A very tight budget. He presented it that way, and over time we figured out how to make it work financially for both of us. I don't think I ever met Barry in that context. I'm not sure. It was all Marshall. It wasn't until I started designing it that we met with Barry.

I met with Marshall and his team, Joe Rose and Adam Flatto, and we started working on the zoning. It had to be a two-step building because of the zoning, so at the sixth floor there's a step back. And we did fifty models, studying it. We showed them the models, and then they said they liked this, they liked that. I agonize about materials. I did one model in brick, I did some in glass, I did some in metal. The core had to be right, the stairs had to be right. Then the area is kind of industrial with the development right there of the High Line [the onetime home of an elevated railway, being developed as a park] and the intent in New York City to revere that industrial heritage. By their promotion of the High Line, it gave the signal that they are intending, as a community, to emulate that. So I took all of that into account in the doing of this building.

BI: When did it become clear that Diller wanted a white building?

FG: It was just a product of circumstance. When we build the models, we use plastic. The plastic looks white, and we keep it that way because you can read

A model for IAC's new headquarters building in New York's Chelsea neighborhood

the forms. If you make it in clear glass you lose the quality of the form. He always liked those white models.

We eventually got to the scheme that we all liked, and the scheme emulated sails, and that's when I started to think about his sailboat. It was going to be in the marina there, and so the idea was sailboat aesthetic with the industrial background. It's subtle. It's a feeling thing. I would say to myself, "Well, this is a schooner with all its sails to the wind. So then how do you turn that idea into a white building?"

Gehry pauses at this point to pick up a water glass on the table. He has a point to make.

FG: Glass when it's clear appears dark. Right? It's black. There is a standard way—it's not an invention of ours or anything—of using frit to keep the sun

PHOTO: © ERIC S. LEVIN

Glass panels destined for the IAC building move along the assembly line.

out, and it looks white. I'd used frit in the new Chiat/Day offices in our complex here, and I'd done other things with it before. It's a silk-screened ceramic that's baked in an oven and stays on the glass.

BI: Were you restricted as to how much or what kind of glass you could use?

FG: New York requires an energy calculation, and you have to meet energy codes. So if we had every piece of glass with the dots representing a substantial portion of the piece of glass, and it's solid, you're looking out at the view through dots. It's not a really bad thing. People in their offices are always busy. They're not sitting there just looking at the view, right? It works very well and it gives the appearance of a white glass building.

The only problem was when Barry Diller saw the mock-up, he didn't like looking through the dots. He thought that would be a problem. So then we had to come up with a way of leaving a section clear. When you're sitting down at a desk and you're looking out the window, it had to be clear, and when you're standing up looking out, it had to be clear. So there's a panel that had to be clear. And in order to meet the requirement, we had to grade the dots so in that panel going down and going up, the dots feathered. They became more

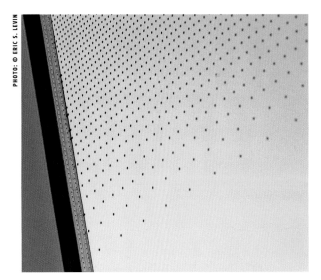

PHOTO: © ERIC S. LEVIN

The IAC building uses frit, a silk-screened ceramic that fuses to the glass.

dense as they went to the bottom and more dense as they went to the top.

BI: Were there problems and trade-offs on that?

FG: Yes. In certain light the building has stripes. And when the building went up with those "stripes," my brothers in architecture said, "Gehry, you screwed up. You failed. It's a terrible-looking building."

So in order to offset that, which my brethren didn't know, is first of all, from the inside it never was opaque. When you're inside and you're looking out, you see all the way to the ceiling and all the way to the floor. There are more dots at the bottom and more dots at the top, but it does work really beautifully. And at night, as soon as the lights inside go on, the room is exposed from floor to ceiling, and people outside see it without stripes and more like a lantern.

Because Barry was very worried about a mirror-glass building, I convinced them that if we put a touch of reflectivity in the coating on the glass, it's almost imperceptible and it starts to blur that problem. So when the clouds go over and there are reflections on the glass, the stripes are muddied—you don't see them as definitively. Lights inside, which are on all day, also blur things. So when you walk by the building, even though you can look at it and see stripes, it's not a striped building. That was what I was doing, and that's what made it work. It was pretty subtle actually.

BI: This is your first completed building in New York. Was it more difficult to deal with codes and all that in New York?

FG: No. And you have to know that the idea that it's my first building in New York wasn't in my head. I don't really care that much. I wasn't ravenous to do my first building in New York. I didn't go out of my way. If for my

During the day, the IAC building has "stripes" in certain light. During the evening, the "stripes" yield to a lanternlike appearance.

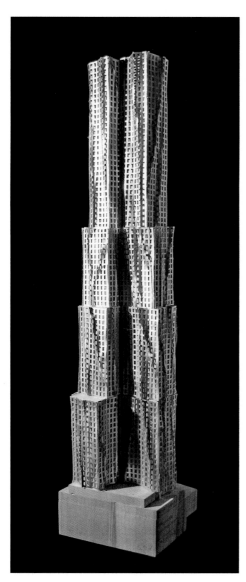

Model for Beekman Tower in New York

whole life the most important thing was to do a building in New York, I would have worked at that. But I didn't, and it isn't. It still isn't. I love New York, but I don't care.

BI: This is a general feeling of yours about longing for things, isn't it?

FG: One's life can't be held hostage to that kind of idea. I've never felt that way. Sure, I wanted to do a concert hall in downtown LA, but I didn't crawl up the stairs to the cardinal to pray for it. If it happened, it happened. There are things I'd love to do. I'd love to do a little hotel in Ireland.

BI: Let's stay with New York for a minute. It's been a couple of decades since you were designing a town house there for [the art collector and designer] Christophe de Menil. That didn't have a very happy ending.

FG: I worked very hard with Christophe de Menil on her town house. It was a big deal. We worked on it a lot. I would fly to New York, spend two or three days with her, and she'd come out here. It went on and on. A lot of effort was invested in it. Then, one day I went to her house, and when we started talking about the plans, she was feisty and negative about me and the things I was doing. You have to understand that it was such a worked-over design. She was always changing it, and I was trying to keep up with her changes and feelings about it. That day she talked about changing big parts of the town house, and I said, "That means you don't want me to do this anymore?" And she said, "Yes." I said, "Do you want me to leave?" She said, "Yes." So I walked out the door, just like that, right away, and got a cab. I'd invested so much time in it, and it was going to be a failure. What did I do wrong? And before I could collect my thoughts about what went wrong, I just burst into tears.

BI: Did you learn something from that experience?

FG: Yes. I just didn't fit there. It's not my thing. I originally went into city planning at Harvard because I didn't want to do rich guys' houses, and it all came back to me. I don't accept house commissions anymore.

BI: Now you're back in New York with several projects, including the new Beekman Tower under construction in downtown Manhattan. What sparked that design?

FG: I used to stay at the Four Seasons Hotel when I was in New York, and just after we got the Beekman project, I was there for meetings. I decided to stay two extra days, and I asked for a room on a high floor so I could look at the buildings. I just stared out the window at them, trying to understand the typology of New York City a little better. I also walked around the city a lot and looked at the buildings from street level and came to conclusions that were used to build Beekman. I think that's why Beekman has that look. Josep Acebillo, a friend of mine who is the chief architect of Barcelona, was here a little while ago, and he said his favorite building model in my office was Beekman, because when he looked at it, he knew *exactly* where it was going to be built without my telling him.

BI: There's also the playground in Battery Park. And you designed the concert hall at Bard College up the Hudson.

FG: There isn't much to say yet about the playground. A friend in New York asked me if I would be interested in doing a children's playground in that area, and I said, "Well, I can't, our fees are too high." But I realized I was doing the Beekman Tower downtown and the work in Brooklyn, and I thought it

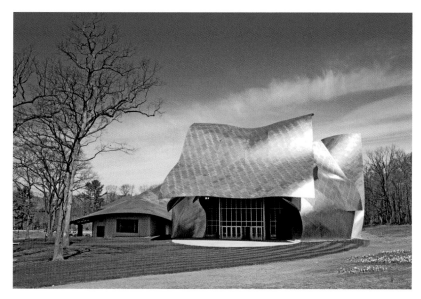

The Richard B. Fisher Center for the Performing Arts at Bard College opened in New York's Hudson Valley, about ninety miles north of Manhattan, in 2003.

would be a nice gesture to give something back. This seemed like the right thing to do, so I'm doing it pro bono. The office team likes it and we have some ideas for it, working with MIT Robotics, among others.

BI: At Bard College, the Fisher Center seems to fit so well with its Hudson Valley setting.

FG: The Fisher Center's exterior grew out of the site, where you come across a meadow to the building. You see it from the distance, and the stainless steel reflects the sky, so on a gray day the form just disappears into the sky. I played with that idea in California many years ago on the hay barn at Donna O'Neill's ranch in San Juan Capistrano and then on the Ron Davis house in Malibu. But at Bard I did it with a vengeance, and it does work when you go there. In fact, if you go when it's snowing, it's just magical. Everything is kind of ephemeral, and you're not quite sure whether it's a building or not.

BI: What was the origin of that commission?

Gehry used wood at Bard and in the Walt Disney Concert Hall because "it psychologically enhances the feeling of the music."

FG: [President of Bard College] Leon Botstein wanted me to do something at Bard [in Annandale-on-Hudson], so I visited him with the idea of doing a student union or something. But he had decided that I should do a small concert hall, and since there were theater and dance programs, it was a little complex to relate to the performing arts. Leon conducts the American Symphony and they would use it for concerts, and it would also be part of the music school, so it would be a teaching facility. It also had to be multiuse, because [the stage director] JoAnne Akalaitis was there and would use it for theater.

BI: You also chose wood for the interior.

FG: You want to break down the barrier between the listener and what he or she is listening to or seeing in the theater. I used wood, like in Disney Hall, because it psychologically enhances the feeling of the music. People relate to musical instruments that are made of wood, like the violins and the cellos. It doesn't have to be wood—wood is just the decoration—but it does have a psychological effect on people listening to music.

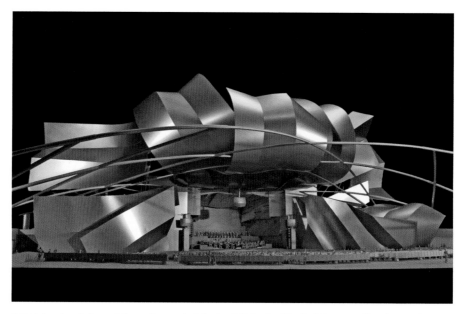

A model and a photograph (opposite page) of the Jay Pritzker Pavilion in Chicago's Millennium Park

The funny thing about it is that when you design something with nine hundred or a thousand seats at a college, you think of a small hall which would have maybe eighty musicians at a time onstage. We designed it with an orchestra pit so they could do chamber opera, and with the capability of taking out the musical shell for opera. But all of us thought that because of the scale of the school and project, the program given to us would stay in those modest ranges and they wouldn't be doing big Mahler pieces.

Then, three months before the opening, Leon calls me all excited that his first concert is going to be Mahler's Symphony No. 3, and I thought I'd have a heart attack. When I called [the acoustician] Yasuhisa Toyota, *he* had a heart attack. So I called Leon back and asked him if he could start with something smaller than Mahler. When he got mad at me and asked, "You mean this doesn't work for Mahler?" I replied, "I'm not saying that. I'm saying it's a difficult thing to start with, to break in a hall. I'm sure it can work, but the hall wasn't designed for that, because Mahler 3 has a chorus of about 300 people. It has 110 musicians. And it's pretty loud. The building couldn't possibly be big enough to do it comfortably."

BI: How was it resolved?

FG: He got his way. We did Mahler 3. I was there, and there were two passages where I thought my ears were going to split open, the pressure from the sound was so great. Toyota cracked open the acoustical shell, so that he increased the volume of the backstage into the fly gallery, to take some of the pressure off it, and it worked. People liked it. In those two passages, it got heavy, but everybody lived through it, and it was a great performance. So it all worked out.

BI: The Pritzker Pavilion in Chicago's Millennium Park followed Disney Hall and Fisher pretty closely. How did Pritzker come about?

FG: I was approached by a Chicago architect to do a façade for a music pavilion in Millennium Park, and I turned it down. I didn't hear about it again until six months had passed and some people from the mayor's office came to see me and said they wanted me to do something related to Millennium Park. I said I'd already turned down the idea of a façade. When they replied that it was very important for them to have me do something in the park, I told them that while I didn't want to do a façade, I'd be happy to do a building. They said, "Okay, you can do the building." So then I asked, "What's your schedule?" And they said, "Well it has to be done for the year 2000, for the Millennium." Since that was eighteen months away, I said, "That's impossible." So they said, "Okay, when can you have it done?" Same thing when I asked them the budget. They gave me a low figure, I said, "You can't do it for that," and again, they said, "Okay. What is the budget?"

At that point, I looked at them and said, "You're too easy. Everything I'm saying, you're willing to concede. What aren't you guys telling me?" And when they replied, "Cindy," I got it.

BI: Cindy?

FG: Cindy Pritzker. Cindy Pritzker was apparently putting up the money for the family to name it the Jay Pritzker Pavilion, and she was a real old friend of mine. So once they said that, I understood and I accepted the project.

BI: What led to that distinctive overhead trellis?

FG: After I visited the site, met with the people involved, and got the program, I felt they had to have a time-delay speaker system in order to make it a significant venue for listening to music.

There had to be a speaker every seventy feet. One alternative was to put a speaker at the top of every post. Then, as you sat on the lawn and listened to music, you'd be in a forest of posts. I felt that was not a good way to do it, and so I came up with the idea of a trellis in which the speakers were hung so that the trellis formed a kind of sky. The trellis identified and created a sense of space, and the sound distribution system works.

BI: I assume this was a more expensive alternative?

FG: I think it was a three-million-dollar premium to go from the posts to the trellis. When I explained it to the mayor, I said, "You're close to making a really important venue, and if you do this, even the Chicago Symphony will want to play here." That got reported in the press, and the Grant Park Symphony that we were designing the pavilion for was insulted by my remark. It was as if I'd said they weren't good enough to play there, which is not what I meant.

BI: *Does* the Chicago Symphony play there?

FG: Yes, and so does the Grant Park Orchestra. [Since it opened in July 2004,] it's been successful as a venue and as an identity, and the real estate values have skyrocketed around it.

BI: Which brings us to your hall for the New World Symphony in Miami, which started construction in January 2008, for [the conductor and San Francisco Symphony music director] Michael Tilson Thomas.

FG: I've been friends with Michael since he was eight years old; in fact, I babysat for him several times when he was a kid, and we'd stayed friends over the years. He was a precocious genius even at eight and continued to grow musically into a great master. I have great respect for him, so when he called and asked me to do the new concert hall in Miami, I was thrilled.

A model for the New World Symphony in Miami. Gehry babysat the NWS founder and artistic director, Michael Tilson Thomas, long, long ago.

GEHRY BUILDS A DOGHOUSE

Construction proceeds on the Lou Ruvo Brain Institute, a project which is particularly meaningful to Gehry. Situated in downtown Las Vegas, the institute will include research, treatment, and other facilities for Alzheimer's, Parkinson's, and Huntington's diseases and related illnesses. Gehry has been active for several decades with the Hereditary Disease Foundation in Los Angeles.

BI: I haven't heard much from you recently about the Lou Ruvo Brain Institute you're designing in Las Vegas.

FG: Maybe it has to do with aging, and I don't dwell on it, but from time to time it does occur to me that I'm running out of time. There's not much I can do about the buildings and things that are done. My excitement and what keeps me going is what I'm working on *now*. I'm involved with clients, and I've got groundbreakings and openings and all that, but it's difficult to go backwards and talk about things even from the current past, like the Ruvo building, which is under construction.

BI: Since the Ruvo Institute is going to research neurological disorders, maybe we could talk about it in the context of the Hereditary Disease Foundation that psychoanalyst Milton Wexler founded to investigate Huntington's disease and related disorders.

FG: [The artist] Ed Moses took me to see Milton when I was struggling with my first marriage. I was acting strange and self-destructive, and Milton helped me a lot.

It was during the time I was getting help from him that I found out about how Milton started the foundation in 1968 when his wife was diagnosed with Huntington's. Several of his patients and friends got involved with him and were on the foundation's board. Many of us were well known, and we helped him raise money, attended fund-raising parties. I think we gave weight to the foundation and credibility for the scientists to be involved. They could feel there was a support system.

BI: At one point, wasn't the foundation going to build something?

FG: In the 1970s, right at the beginning, Milton said, "We need to build a facility for research. And since you're a part of the foundation, we'd like you to be the architect." I needed the work at that point, and the idea of doing something like that as a project was kind of exciting.

Then they had a meeting about it. Milton told me later that the scientists voted to have an institute without walls and, as a result, there was no need for a building. I said, "You mean I got fired already?" But I understood, and they have existed like that, very efficiently, for many years now. They became affiliated with laboratories that were already in existence all over the world, and having offices would have been antithetical to that. You could do it all by telephone, and now with e-mail. You don't really need a place, so we never had one.

A model for the Lou Ruvo Brain Institute in downtown Las Vegas

BI: You've remained on the board all these years, haven't you?

FG: I'm vice president of the board. Berta is on the board, too.

BI: Which brings us to the Ruvo project.

FG: First, let me put it in context. Before Larry Ruvo called me, I turned down every project that came to me for Las Vegas. There were three or four big, big ones, but I just couldn't see myself doing that. It's not that I'm against gambling. My father sold slot machines. Pinball machines. It was the carny business, and I grew up in that, so I wasn't judgmental. But the few times I had been to Vegas, I'd seen all those people, like lemmings, sitting in front of slot machines for hours, putting money in. I think it's a substitute for sex for those people. It's the titillation they need. It seemed so negative that I just didn't want to be part of it. I couldn't imagine designing a place that would contribute to those needs. When I design a building, I want to feel like I'm contributing something.

So then along comes Larry Ruvo. He knows that I've turned everything down. He knows that I'm not interested in Las Vegas. But he wants to meet with me and discuss it anyway, so he came to the office. He's the senior managing director of Southern Wine & Spirits of Nevada, which means he's the liquor distributor for Vegas. He hangs out with the Vegas developer Steve Wynn and all those guys. He felt okay to me because of my father and the kind of people my dad hung around with. I felt comfortable with him, and I quite liked him. Larry's father, who the center is named after, was a victim of Alzheimer's disease, and I talked with Larry about Milton and the foundation. We're also terrible fund-raisers at our foundation, and this guy, who is raising five million dollars at a dinner, tells me, "If you take this job, I'll have one big dinner in Vegas and raise five or six million for your foundation."

BI: Has that happened?

FG: He hasn't done it yet, but he talks about it. He reminds me of it, so I suspect sometime he'll do it. And he put in the building program "Offices for the Hereditary Disease Foundation" as a gesture.

He brought all these characters from Vegas here—the mayor, Oscar Goodman, Tony Curtis, I don't know who else. I met Tony Curtis's daughter, Jamie Lee Curtis, and I knew Janet Leigh a long time ago. So it became kind of family. And Larry gets close to you. He starts bringing thousand-dollar bottles of wine to me and sends me champagne. He flies in and brings me a case of the best wine in the world. I never asked him for any of this stuff, but he's that kind of guy. He's always doing something. He grew up with Sinatra, and his family restaurant was Sinatra's hangout; I've actually got a tape that Sinatra made for his birthday.

BI: I've read about how you've helped out with fund-raising for the Ruvo center.

FG: The first time I went was for a big dinner, when he asked me to be honored with [California First Lady] Maria Shriver. Before dinner, he tells me, "This is a good time to relax. You don't have to do anything. We'll pick you up on time for the dinner. Oh, and there are a few things for you to sign."

I go into a room filled with my Cloud Lamps. They're in cardboard boxes. You had to open each box, take the lamp out, sign it, put it back in the box, and put it in a pile. It was three or four hours' worth of signing, and it totally wiped me out. The second year I went to the dinner, I didn't sign them.

BI: Didn't you also design a doghouse as a result of one of his fund-raisers?

FG: Yes. I was sitting there with my family and Milton's daughter, Nancy Wexler, and we had had a few drinks. I'm told they're figuring out all kinds of things to auction, getting a million dollars for this and a million dollars for that. They ask, "Frank, would you do a doghouse?" And I said, "Sure, yes, what the hell. I'll do a doghouse." So someone starts auctioning off the doghouse, and I'm not paying any attention, and there are two guys bidding on it. They're up to $350,000, and they ask me, "Would you do two of them?" By then I'd had another drink, so I said, "Okay, two doghouses." I thought, Fine, I just had to do a sketch.

Then I had to go see the dogs. One of the bidders has two little dogs, but the other guy needs a doghouse the size of my office. So I do the sketches and send them off, and guess what? We have to do the working drawings, and we have

This sketch (above) and model (opposite) show another view
of the Lou Ruvo Brain Institute.

to get them built. We have to supervise everything. It turned out it cost *me* $350,000, that little episode. It's taken time to get them done, and they're all mad at me because I didn't get it done faster.

BI: What makes you say yes to projects now? God knows you don't have the time.

FG: Well, since I turned it all off with the Rouse Company in 1978, I have been very careful which projects I take. I have to like the people, and I have to like the project. There has to be something that I'm interested in or a site I'm interested in.

BI: Wasn't the site one of the things that intrigued you about designing the new museum campus in Biloxi, Mississippi, for the work of potter George Ohr?

FG: Yes, it was. The Ohr-O'Keefe Museum of Art has been a very special project. It has implications of city building, because it's a group of buildings, and it has a specific site requirement of preserving the venerable old trees which are already on the site. So I took the tack of the architecture dancing with the trees. It was quite far along when [Hurricane] Katrina hit, and it was largely destroyed. It's being rebuilt now.

BI: The site for the Lou Ruvo center also appealed to you, didn't it?

FG: This one I called "the mouse that roared" because it was so tiny and in that mess of stuff they've got downtown. Las Vegas is a kind of social aberration. I understand how it got there, but I don't especially want to spend much time there.

BI: Well, how often will you have to go back to Las Vegas when you're doing this?

FG: Probably there'll be a party when it opens, and then I'm through.

BI: That's it?

FG: Yes. Unless Larry gets involved with our Hereditary Disease Foundation in some way.

BI: How often do you go back to your other buildings? You went to Bilbao for the tenth anniversary, for instance. How many times have you been there since it opened?

Gehry's design for a doghouse brought in $350,000 at a
Lou Ruvo charity auction.

FG: Three or four. And that's because we did the hotel at the [Marqués de Riscal] winery near there. Otherwise, I probably wouldn't have gone, although I love the people there. I feel close to them.

I go to Disney Hall all the time. It's probably the only one I really use. Besides my house.

BI: When you're at Disney Hall, do you ever obsess about things that you'd like to have done differently?

FG: For the first two years, I saw everything I wanted to change and it drove me nuts, and I drove the Los Angeles Philharmonic president, Deborah Borda, nuts. I even called Esa-Pekka Salonen, and she got mad at me for doing that. She wrote me a nasty letter. "Don't you mess with the music director."

But then, after a while, I just gave up. It's like you flail against the windmills for a while and then you give up. At Disney Hall, there was someone who decided how the lighting should be. I don't care about the lighting onstage, but he was lighting the corridors, so the doors in the corridors during a concert were lit and bright. I had designed the lighting so it didn't interfere, and every time I went, the damn thing was lit bright. I couldn't stand it.

BI: Did they change it?

To preserve "the venerable old trees which are already on the site," says Gehry, he opted for "architecture dancing with the trees" for the new campus of the Ohr-O'Keefe Museum of Art in Biloxi, Mississippi.

FG: Yes, for a while. Some days it's one way, and some days it's another. It's not consistent. And the skylights. I designed the skylights for Sunday afternoon concerts, and they'll close the back window on the skylights. You ask, "Why do they do that?" Well, they're preparing for the next week's concerts where they have to close them, and apparently it costs money to open and close them. So they leave them closed during a Sunday afternoon concert, which just doesn't make sense. I get furious with that.

The other thing is that I designed the hall in stone, because at night stone would glow. Disney Hall would look beautiful at night in stone. It would have just been great. It would have been friendly. Metal at night goes dark. I begged them. No, after they saw Bilbao, they had to have metal.

BI: Wasn't it to save money?

FG: Well, they used money on me. They wanted to save five million dollars.

BI: And the resulting problems with the reflection from the hall's roof heating up the street and apartments nearby to very high temperatures?

A sketch and model (opposite page) for the luxury Hotel Marqués de Riscal in Elciego, Spain

FG: The reflection wasn't my fault. I told them that would happen. I was taking the heat for all that. It made the list of the ten worst engineering disasters in the decade. I saw it on television, the History Channel. I was number ten.

Gehry is very agitated. These are not idle grievances.

FG: Then they came and told me they had to light the building because I didn't light the metal. Well, I did have a whole system for lighting the metal, and they value-engineered it out. So now the Music Center needs to light the metal, and they bring in their lighting guys. I don't like the way it's lit at night.

And that little amphitheater in the back? It was never covered, and you need shade. But that was value-engineered out. They didn't want to do it. So they hire somebody to design a whole backstage thing with shade and then they sent it to me to approve, because they didn't want it built unless I said it was okay. And it was a total affront to the building. How they could even imagine doing anything like that? So I got mad and I called John Emerson, the Music Center chairman, and I asked him, "Do you realize what they're doing?" So now we're redoing the thing in the back the way we want, for free. But this is the kind of continuing insult, one after another, that goes on for a building that everybody should be appreciating. There should be a sense of

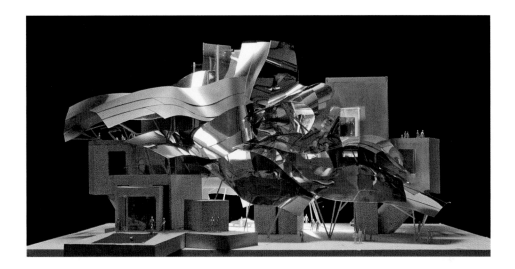

appreciation and respect, but there isn't. God bless them. I know they mean well.

BI: Maybe they have different motivations than you do.

FG: I guess. But it means that over the years, their motivations will lead to a visual denigration of the building, and thirty years from now you probably won't recognize it. That's my guess. They may even decide to tear it down. Obviously it doesn't work for them. They have to do all these things. I've had so many buildings torn down this year that I'm beginning to wonder.

BI: When they tear something down, does that make you feel awful? Or have you let go?

FG: I let go. Kind of.

BI: Do you also let go if it doesn't happen? Like the expansion of the Corcoran Gallery of Art in Washington, or the new Guggenheim for downtown New York? The unbuilt?

FG: I don't obsess over those.

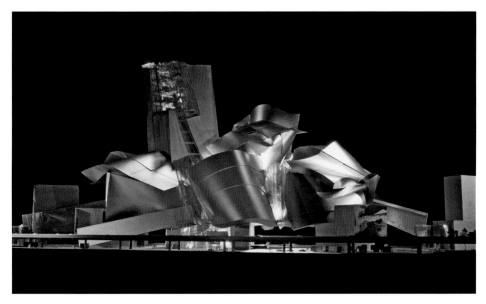

Plans for the proposed Guggenheim Museum in downtown New York did not come to fruition. Neither did the Gehry-designed expansion of the Corcoran Gallery of Art in Washington, D.C. (opposite page).

Gehry is hardly listening to me at this point, however. He's flipping through books, trying to find photographs of Disney Hall that make him crazy. Disney Hall in full metal. Eventually he finds one.

FG: Look at this. Darth Vader in *Star Wars*. Compared to the stone.

BI: But that building is gorgeous.

FG: It's just that it would have been better. Imagine if it were stone. Think about how beautiful it would be.

BI: Isn't compromise something you deal with all the time?

FG: I think that the world lives with compromise, so most of the concert halls that have been built since the war are compromised, and they needn't have been. And most of the art museums built since the war are compromised, and they needn't have been.

BI: Why does that happen, in your opinion?

FG: There's kind of a wrong-headed system of how architects are selected, how they're paid, and how they're worked with. We did the Guggenheim Bilbao and it was a hit, right? But nobody called us for another one. As nearly as I can tell, the reason they don't call for another one is they assume you're going to do a museum that looks exactly like that one. They want their own, and they'll settle for less sometimes so they can have their own. That's more important to them than having a proven track record.

BI: Does this happen a lot to you?

FG: We run into it all the time. You can't say, "Hey, wait a minute. I just did this great concert hall. What are you talking about? I can do another one. I'll make it even better." That isn't the game. A lot of other people have gotten concert halls all over the place, and we haven't.

Disney Hall *really* works. As I said, it's the one building that I've done, other than my house, that I really use. I love classical music and I spend a lot of time there. And I know it works because I can hear the bass clearly, and the separa-

Stone and metal models for the Walt Disney Concert Hall

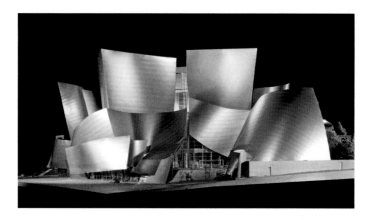

tion of instruments, which has always been something that people have talked about in terms of halls they find "too muddy." There's a clarity at Disney Hall. I experienced it when I went to Vienna's Musikverein for the first time, but nowhere else have I experienced that.

I went to hear Gustavo Dudamel conduct at Disney Hall the other night. Imagine Mahler 5 and Beethoven 5, played Latin American style, but without trivializing or caricaturing either. We're going from sad wintry nights in Finland with Esa-Pekka Salonen to salsa with Dudamel. I was talking to Dudamel's manager, who asked me if I had done another major concert hall, and I said no. The ones at Bard College and coming up in Miami are small.

Even in Bilbao, they've done a lot of buildings since we did the Guggenheim, but they've never asked us to do another building. And when we ask about it, we're told, "Well, we already have a Frank Gehry." On Bilbao, too, a lot of reporters claim it doesn't work for art. But if you talk to the curators and Tom Krens and the Basques, it works great for art and the artists love it.

BI: What do you think is going on?

FG: People look at the buildings finished, and the implication is that it had to be designed as a figment of my imagination, and that it has nothing to do with function or respect for neighbors or anything. And then, miraculously, I've been lucky to push the program into it and somehow gerrymander it so it works, after the fact. That is the perception. And they don't acknowledge the fifty or sixty models, the agony about meeting budgets and time schedules, the technical issues and all those things that are part of the mix of work going to the finale.

The whole thing about being an artist is that people think you're not businesslike: "We big developers know how to do it," blah, blah, blah. So I pride myself that I run a tight ship. Some high-powered people, the few that I've let into the show, ask how I do it. Well, it's important that it run like that because if you're going to work for people, they need to feel like they're connected to a responsible base. If it's totally irresponsible and wacko, they're at risk.

When you hire an architectural firm and it's managed poorly, it costs you, because you don't get the service. Talk to Bruce Ratner or Marshall Rose. They've had twenty architects working for them, and ours deliver the best product. Forget about the design for a minute. I'm talking about being on time, on budget, and responsible, all the things that the general public thinks aren't true. Irresponsible reporters don't take the time to find that out, and instead create innuendo about how I'm a flake. There's a lot of that still in the press, you know.

People think that somebody who does this kind of out-there work that they haven't seen before must be irresponsible and must not be interested in budgets or time schedules or the client, or the community that the building is going to be in. They characterize it as an ego trip by superstar architects. Now in some cases it may be true, but it's not in mine.

Even Gehry is impressed with the "clarity" of sound in the Walt Disney Concert Hall's auditorium.

It's no accident that Disney Hall works. Ernest Fleischmann could tell you what happened. Did Ernest tell you how I listened to him?

BI: Yes, he did tell me that. In fact, several people I've interviewed recently said that one of your best traits is that you listen. I was just reading remarks by Matthew Teitelbaum, director of the Art Gallery of Ontario, who said that from the very beginning you "insistently asked" about the museum's needs and programming.

FG: So put that in big letters: Gehry is a listener. He is *not* on an ego trip.

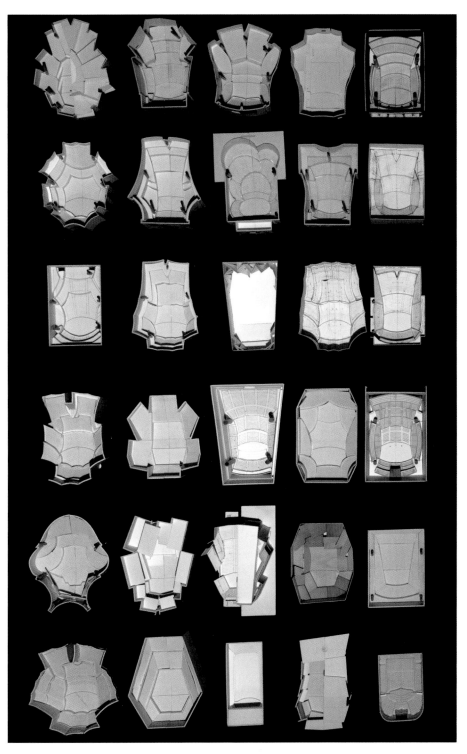

Gehry may make dozens of models, like these for Disney Hall, in designing a building.

Life occasionally comes full circle for Gehry. There is, for example, his expansion of Toronto's Art Gallery of Ontario, the first museum he ever visited and a fixture in the neighborhood where he grew up. As early as December 2007, a year before it was scheduled to open, it was already a "staggering success" for Toronto Globe and Mail *architecture critic Lisa Rochon. Around the same time, he celebrated the tenth anniversary of the Guggenheim Bilbao and was working again on a project in Paris, a city he loves.*

Similarly, in September 2005, Gehry and his wife, Berta, made a brief visit to Timmins, the mining town in Canada where he spent several difficult years as a boy, between 1937 and 1942. It was the first time he had been back since 1942.

FG: Timmins when I lived there had thirty-five thousand people, and now it has forty-five thousand people. There's been very little change. There are some new buildings but it's still a very small place. Where we lived, you would go to the end of the street and be right in the raw forest. The trees are so solid, you feel that if you walk in, you won't come back out. That kind of forest. And there are bears in those forests. Because we lived on the edge of the bush, we'd hear or see them when they went into the garbage cans looking for food. Or we'd run into them when we'd go pick wild blueberries, which are all over the forest and which the bears also like. They're scary, but usually they run away when you come near them.

BI: What prompted you to return to Timmins?

FG: I went back with Frank Mahovlich, one of the greatest hockey players ever and now a Canadian senator. When I got my Order of Canada [consid-

ered "the centerpiece of Canada's system of honors"] a few years ago [in 2003], Frank and his wife,
Marie, came to the ceremony, along with the actor
Donald Sutherland and his wife, Francine Racette.
At that ceremony Marie told me Frank was born
in Schumacher, which is one mile from Timmins,
and he lived in Timmins as a kid. I didn't know
him then, but it turns out he lived two blocks from
where I lived. She said, "Wouldn't it be great if the
two Franks went back to Timmins and Schumacher and had a parade down Main Street?" She
said she could organize it, so I agreed to go.

It took a while to do, but she followed up on it.
And so we flew to Timmins, where the mayor
picked us up in a white stretch limo with someone
in white gloves carrying the Stanley Cup [hockey's
championship trophy]. And for added juice they
brought the World Cup [of Hockey] that I designed
[in 2004]. I wanted to experience how it would feel
to pick up the Stanley Cup and hold it over your

Gehry designed the World Cup
of Hockey trophy in 2004.

head, because it's the thing they all talk about when you design a cup. I wanted
to see how heavy it was in relation to mine. But the fellow with the white
gloves wouldn't let anybody touch it, including me. I tried to, and he said,
"Don't do that!"

Anyway, we got in the stretch limo and drove into Timmins. On the way we
stopped at an old-age home, where people remembered Frank as a hockey
player, and where a 102-year-old woman in a wheelchair winked at me. They
were all so happy to see Frank and they didn't know who I was, nor did they
care. It became obvious right away that I was excess baggage, and it was fun to
be that. A guy I knew as a kid came because he knew I was going to be there,
since it was in the *Timmins Daily Press,* which I used to sell when I was a boy.

We stopped for a press conference and lunch at the community center in
Schumacher. The press knew I'd lived in Timmins, knew I knew Schumacher, knew I knew hockey, knew I knew Frank Mahovlich, knew this was
the first time I'd been back since 1942, and so you would think they would ask
questions about any of those topics—but they didn't. There were only two or

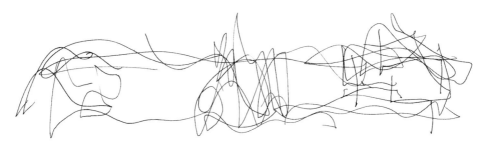

A sketch (above) and models (below) of the Art Gallery of Ontario in Toronto, near where Gehry grew up. The AGO is the first museum he visited.

three questions like "What's your favorite toothpaste?" and that was it. That was the press conference.

Frank wanted me to see the hockey rink there, and when we did, I realized it was the first hockey rink I'd ever played on, and I started to cry. It looked exactly the same. Later I saw another friend I hadn't seen since school, and we talked about the old days a bit.

BI: What do you remember most vividly about those old days?

FG: There were thirty Jewish families—today there are eight—and all of us huddled together. There was a synagogue, and that's where the social life of our community took place. Jewish families owned the lumber mill, the car dealership, the department stores. The Goldbergs, my parents, were poor, but they were taken in by that community because they were Jewish. We were invited to everything, and I played with the other Jewish kids and, in fact, still have contact with some of them. I studied with the rabbis in Timmins for my bar mitzvah, which I then had in Toronto, because my grandparents were in Toronto.

We were there when Hitler was rising to power, so I remember hearing his speeches on the radio. We were scared about it, and anti-Semitism was pretty heavy. I was the only Jew at the Birch Street Elementary School, and kids would harass me in the schoolyard or on the ice rink at recess, and when I was eleven or twelve, there was one kid who used to follow me home. Every time he caught me, he would pummel me. Then one day I turned on the guy and beat *him* up. I just had had enough. After that, we would alternate who beat up who, and, finally, we became friends. We had something in common: we beat each other up.

BI: Did you have a chance to go back to places you remembered from your childhood?

FG: I went to find the synagogue where I'd gone as a kid, and it had been torn down, but our old house was still there. They took me to see it and they took us to see the house Frank lived in, and we realized we really *were* neighbors. Mahovlich went to the house he lived in, knocked on the door, and talked to the people. I couldn't bring myself to do that. Where he had lived, they were excited to see him because they knew he had lived there. But I was sure that the people who were in my house wouldn't even know who I was. I would have had to stand there and give them a lot of explanation before they'd start to get it, so I didn't bother.

BI: Even without going in, did looking at your old house bring back any feelings or thoughts about that time?

FG: I thought of my family, but it also made me realize—which I didn't realize when I was a kid there—how barren a place Timmins is. It was a tiny mining town. The mine's gone now, and I don't know what sustains it. I went to the river that I used to swim in. Like everything else, it looked smaller. Going there sort of put something to rest. When we left, we all said we'd be back, but I'll never go back there.

BI: Going back to Toronto to work on the Art Gallery of Ontario [AGO] expansion is presumably quite a different experience for you.

FG: I was eight years old when I first went to the AGO with my mother, and I remember the nearby park where I used to play and the synagogue where I had my bar mitzvah. My uncles lived nearby.

BI: Had you been back there much before this project?

FG: I did some teaching at the University of Toronto, and I gave a talk at the University of Waterloo, which is a couple hours from Toronto. There was a show of my work at the Toronto Art Centre, and the University of Toronto gave me an honorary doctorate.

So they were circling the field a lot with me. But I never asked for any work. I never did.

The Toronto Maple Leafs were moving to the Air Canada Centre, and there was a move to preserve their former home, Maple Leaf Gardens. They wanted to do something with it and got me into some of the discussions. So there were things going on.

We were asked to do a proposal for the opera house in Toronto, but when we met with the client group and told them what we thought it would cost per square foot, they were outraged and told the press our opera house was too expensive. So they used a Toronto architect and the opera house cost more than what I told them.

Same with a new cultural center where they didn't want to spend the money and hired a local architect. There was a temple expansion, on which we did some studies, but they couldn't raise the money. They also hired someone local, and guess who they hired? The same guy who did the opera house: Jack Diamond.

All this gives you the context for my feelings about building in Toronto. I had been through the mill, to the point where I didn't believe anybody. Nor was I that interested in getting my feelings beat on one more time by my hometown.

BI: There were some other good things happening before the AGO selection, weren't there?

FG: Well, in the middle of all that, Heather Reisman [founder and CEO of Indigo Books and Music] instigated fund-raising at the University of Toronto to name an endowed chair in architecture for me, so there's now the Frank Gehry International Visiting Chair in Architectural Design at the University of Toronto. And Prime Minister [Jean] Chrétien gave me my Canadian citizenship back. They also gave me the Order of Canada, which is the highest honor they can give [a civilian]. So they've been nice to me, and I hope my building is nice to them.

BI: Do you ever think what might have happened with your career had your family not moved to California when you were a teenager?

FG: I think, had I stayed there, I would have been something else. I really believe that. There are places all over the world where there are talented people who for some reason or other don't fit into the characteristics required to advance in their fields. I think a lot of people are misused in our culture and not given the chance. I think about my own father, who could draw and won awards for window dressing when he was young. He must have had the right-brain stuff that I have. His sister became a famous dress designer in Florida. My mother's side of the family was all lawyers and doctors and businessmen.

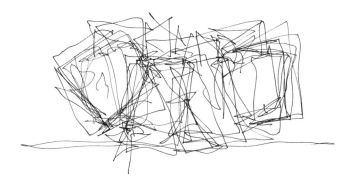

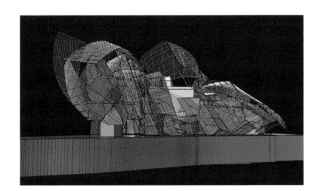

Sketch and models for the Louis Vuitton Foundation for Creation in the Bois de Boulogne in Paris

BI: Any other thoughts about Canada?

FG: They're not used to architecture the way we are. They've put their toe in it. They've got Daniel Libeskind, but the country doesn't nurture high-end architecture. There isn't that much. Bruce Kuwabara and a couple of others. It hasn't been a big topic up there, although it may be changing.

BI: And personally?

FG: I emotionally resonate to the country, to the people, to my history with it. I still have family there. And I feel at home there.

BI: When you received the commission for the Louis Vuitton Foundation for Creation in Paris, you talked quite a bit about your great fondness for that city as well. You were quoted in *Le Monde* calling Paris your favorite city. Actually, you seemed equally enamored of the project itself, saying that when Bernard Arnault, "this man connected to fashion, who collects artworks that I love, asked me to build something in the city, it was like a sign from heaven."

FG: I loved Paris when I lived there, as I've said. At that time, I really wanted to stay and make it home. There was just something about it. Walking the streets. The baguettes. There was a funny edge to the people that I found amusing. It gave you license to be outrageous like they were. They like the banter. For example, they like talking about what they call "the American weakness." We're always weak: I had a pencil sharpener and they used a razor blade. When I left Paris, I took my pencil sharpener apart and gave everyone a separate piece of it. Today we don't even use pencils.

BI: Do you still feel that attachment to Paris?

FG: Paris was always interesting to me and still is to this day.

BI: I recall your excitement about designing the American Center there in the early nineties.

FG: Later, after it opened, it became clear they didn't have the money to run it. It was disappointing. It's now a cinematheque, which required many changes.

BI: Were there things you learned doing the American Center that you could apply to the LVMH project?

FG: I learned how difficult it was to work with the French. They complicate things so much. They get very detail-oriented. They create a bureaucracy even within a private development. They're more individualistic. In places like Sweden and Canada, people are more likely to work in teams.

Gehry pauses, giving this analysis some thought.

FG: Hockey may help.

BI: Had you known Bernard Arnault before this new project for him and the foundation?

FG: I had been in Paris three days before 9/11 to meet with Arnault about doing a store in Japan, which I never got to do. And then I didn't hear from him again until this museum. He drove me to the site at the Jardin d'Acclimatation children's park [in the Bois de Boulogne], and it was so magical. It was a pretty extraordinary commission.

BI: You also feel at home now in Bilbao, don't you? I know you were looking forward to going back there for the tenth anniversary. What was it like?

FG: I always like going there. People are very nice to me, and I have been given all kinds of honors there. But I hadn't been there for a while, and they've done some funny things along the waterfront near my building. They put in some new buildings, and they prettified the landscape. They took a lot of what I liked about the riverfront and changed it. It was very industrial and tough before, and now they've prettied it up. I was disappointed in that.

BI: Do you feel like your part is finished?

FG: Architectural projects have so many facets to them, it's difficult to ever truly finish. You can always find something you want to change or build on or remove or add to or whatever. The discipline of budgets and time and schedules is very important.

BI: We've also talked many times in the past about the importance of change.

FG: Well, we're living in a world that just keeps constantly changing and evolving, and my sense is that it's important to respond to that change. Otherwise, you lose your relationship to the dynamic of it. Now architecture does get frozen at some point. It becomes a static piece, and time goes by. Our hope is that the static piece will have some life in the changing environment.

BI: Ten years later, how did Bilbao look to you?

FG: Well, I got over all of my own criticism of it. I go through a period of a couple years where I just see all the things I would have changed.

BI: Do you do that on everything?

FG: Everything. I'm bad. You'd think when a building is finished I should be grateful and love it, but I don't.

BI: Does it get easier? Or do you think what you do next is as hard as what you did before?

FG: I always thought it was supposed to get easier as you continue working, and in some ways, it does. I'm faster than I ever was in coming to conclusions, but then I question the conclusion, because it happened so fast, and I throw myself into agonizing reappraisal. I think there's a required sense of insecurity that's very positive to the process. It fuels the creative engine and leads you to new places.

I always feel precarious. I don't feel like my work is resolved. It's intuitive and I don't have a road map, so I can't always explain it. I can take pride that Disney Hall works and people like it and like going there. I understand why it works, and I understand why they like it. But I'm never sure until it's over. And then, even when the building is finished, it feels precarious to me. Since it doesn't really look like something else I've seen, I worry that it's some kind of bizarre thing. I feel self-conscious about it, and I want to hide. I want to crawl under the blankets. When I saw Bilbao for the first time, I said, "Oh my God, what have I done to these people?" I think that's a problem, but for better or worse, that's who I am.

BI: Do you acknowledge the success at all, the honors and awards?

FG: I like it all, but I'm oblivious to it. There's always something else to do. I'm trying to solve something and arrive somewhere so I never am in a state of being finished. I finish a building, and then I'm the ingénue again, as frustrated as ever, starting over. I always think what I do next is as hard as what I've done before. Did things change for me after Bilbao? I think better projects were coming in, but I don't relate to it like that. From my perspective, it's all hard.

BI: Especially now, it seems, given that in addition to the various smaller projects you're working on, you're also tackling those huge projects in LA and New York at the same time. How do you do that?

FG: I don't know. We get it done. I don't do all of it.

BI: But you're always involved, since it's coming from Gehry Partners.

FG: You know, I always thought the office was my ego trip. Since I was doing the design, I thought that people were here to assist me in creating whatever the design is for whoever the client is. And so I've always acted like they were doing me a favor, even though I was paying them. I tended to be overly generous in my dealings with the staff, both financially and manageri-ally. When design guys like me are starting out, we have trouble getting tech-nical people to sign on, because, first of all, the work doesn't look real in the front end.

BI: You mean people think you'll never get something strange like that built?

Guggenheim Bilbao

FG: You see the model of Disney Hall, and you ask: "How are you going to do that?" So it's hard to get people to sign on—with their lives and families and responsibilities—to what they perceive as being a deckhand on a weird ship. It took a long time to get those technical people.

BI: I assume Gehry Technologies and your experiments with computer software have attracted some of those technical people.

FG: Our purpose, which is kind of an idealistic goal, is to change the profession of architecture, so architects like us aren't marginalized like they are now. Run-of-the-mill architects have developed their relationships with business and society. They seem comfortable with it, and look a little askance at what we do.

Dassault Systems [the software developer], with whom we created a partnership relationship to do this, is interested in the commerce side, and we figure, Well, okay, we would be interested in the commerce a little bit, too, and Gehry Technologies was launched in 2002. Basically—and I'm sort of on shaky ground here in describing it—the software represents the components of the building to seven decimal points of accuracy. That allows us during the design process to analyze our models for surface area, floor area, volume—the kind of things that are the basic elements of cost control. You can analyze structure, mechanical systems, and electrical systems. You can also organize the projects, and you can convey the information very precisely to the construction companies.

It's not just us doing this. Because we were with Dassault and because our buildings are complicated, we are out in front. But I think that's just temporary. I think we have this window, after which the rest of the industry will catch up. It's a very competitive industry, and there are big companies already in the field. They aren't doing it the way we're doing it, but they're sure looking at us.

BI: Put the commerce aside for a second. What's the philosophy behind it?

FG: First of all, I think that the American Institute of Architects is sort of a professional club, which has over the years created documents and processes that protect its members. Inadvertently, I think, they've become overprotec-

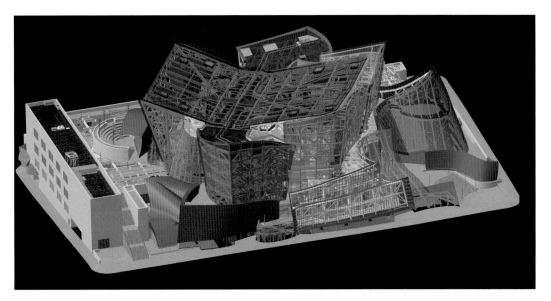

A computer model of Disney Hall

tive, and what happens when you overprotect a child is that you infantilize the child. This is an exaggeration, but I think it basically is true. So architects, in being protected, take less and less responsibility.

BI: How long has this been going on?

FG: Thirty years? Forty years? You can understand why because construction lawsuits are huge. They can destroy a person financially.

BI: So what happened to make you take action?

FG: I realized, by accident really, that the computer let us own a lot more information than any of the other players in the project.

BI: Which then empowers you, the architect?

FG: Here's how it works: The construction team is very happy to get precise information because they'd rather not be guessing. So in a sense, if the architect

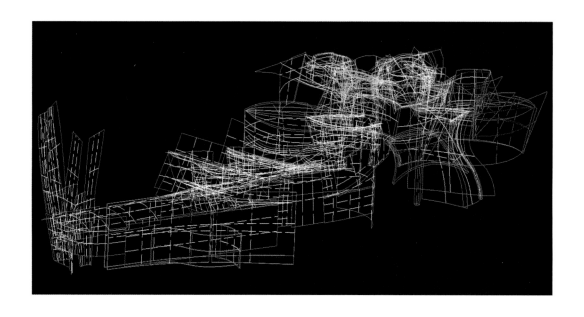

Computer models of Guggenheim Bilbao

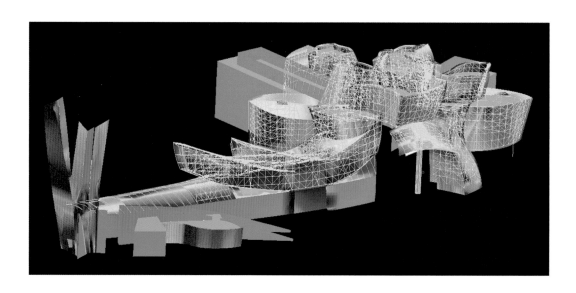

has a tremendous amount of information and can represent it, the architect can become the parent in the equation, and the contractor doesn't mind being the child, as it were, who will take instructions from the parent. It's logical. The architect has developed a project that's in concert with the architect's client, which presumably the client likes, and the only problem is that when it goes out to bid, it's inevitably more money. And by that time it's hard to back out of it, so the client is in a dead end, and the normal thing that happens is the contractor says to the client, "I can take that money out if you'll let me straighten a few walls here and there."

BI: You mean changing the design?

FG: In effect compromising the design. But now, with the computer, you can preempt all of that by having such precise information in advance that the only change in price has to do with the marketplace, which neither the contractor, the architect, nor the client can control. But everything else you can control. You can anticipate steel prices or interest rates going up, for example, and all of that is analyzed during the design process. It makes the architect a partner.

An inevitable subject.

BI: Atlantic Yards and Grand Avenue are both such long-term projects. On these and new work, is there a plan in place about where the office goes after you leave?

FG: Succession is an issue to be grappled with, and we're talking about it. We're talking frankly to clients, so this is not a secret master plan or anything like that. As long as you can have reasonable discussions with people, you can probably sort out a way to work forward. So that's what we're trying to do.

BI: You or the office?

FG: There are two issues in the succession. One is what I should be doing for the rest of my life, and the other is what Gehry Partners as an entity going forward should be doing for the rest of its life. We're trying to find a way to make them not conflict. In a way, if I do what's best for me, it might not end up best for them. But if I try too hard to make the office best for them, I may subvert things that would be best for me, and that might subvert doing some damn good projects.

BI: It's a conundrum.

FG: It is. It's difficult. I think about it a lot, and I talk to the guys about it a lot.

BI: When did you start thinking about this?

FG: A long time ago. More than a decade. When I made my fee separate from the office fee, that was in preparation for this. I don't make a big deal out of it because it's hard to lock yourself into something. I'm trying to keep it flexible. But what I have tried to do, and what I think will be good for the guys, is separate my plans and my retirement needs from their responsibility in the future.

BI: What do you mean, "from their responsibility"?

FG: Well, I'm not sure I can do this, but it means that if I leave tomorrow, they don't have to support me until I die. Usually when the principal like me leaves, it's built into the system that they have to pay him off. I'm trying to set it up so they don't have to do that, because that's an albatross.

I've been fortunate over the years to have people who stay, people who are design talents. The good news is they have been here working with me long enough that we have a very pleasant working relationship. There's a lot of fun in designing buildings, and the relationships continue that. But since it's my office and people pay for my services and expect me to be responsible, I have to make sure of what goes out of here. And when you do that, you don't let the others make mistakes. So they can't learn. In order for them to grow, they have to make their own mistakes, and how do they make their own mistakes within the context of working with me where I'm responsible to the client to deliver a Frank Gehry non-mistake?

So it's hard. The way I work it is they go pretty far and I coach them, but I don't stop them. It's a little slower, and occasionally—which is promising—they get there on their own. My hope is that eventually they will get there on their own without me, completely. They won't need me, and they can deliver the level of work that our clients expect. Sometimes it's happening, and sometimes it's not.

BI: What about when you're the client, like on your new house in Venice?

FG: Berta and I may wind up staying in our Santa Monica house and not moving to a new house after all. There are three parcels of land on the property in Venice, and I'm thinking about dividing it up among my son Sam, who has been working with me and is studying architecture, my chief of staff, the architect Meaghan Lloyd, and Anand Devarajan, a young Gehry Partners architect. I was thinking about the next generation and helping them get

Gehry was selected to build the Serpentine Gallery's annual temporary pavilion in London for summer 2008, a project he worked on with his son Sam. He joins the roster of such prior pavilion architects as Rem Koolhaas and Zaha Hadid.

started. The fun of it now is watching the three of them working together. They all like each other, and they could each design a house on spec, or develop their own architectural firm of young designers and get rid of me.

BI: I went to hear Thom Mayne speak just after he won the Pritzker Prize, and he said a couple of things that you've said as well. One was that architects tend not to get recognized or get really good work until they're older, often in their fifties or sixties.

FG: It takes a long time for people to trust you and for you to develop a unique language. You also have to develop a way of building that unique language so it doesn't leak, so it can be done on budget and all of that. It takes a while. So by the time you get there, you're in your late fifties or sixties. And that's the tradition. Louis Kahn didn't get anything until he was in his late fifties. I think Frank Lloyd Wright was the same. Corbusier. Mies van der Rohe. It's just a profession that peaks later. Then it's over so fast.

Gehry pauses, rephrasing his concern.

FG: Do you think after I die people will realize I was a better guy than they thought I was?

BI: I don't know how to answer that one.

FG: The reason I ask something like that is you wonder how long you have to slog at it. Architecture is a group effort. It relates to a city or a time. It relates to clients and other people. The culture changes. The stock market goes up and down. If there is a recession now, we'll all be hurting, including me. The work will dry up like a desert lake.

I've been through it two or three times already. There's a lot more going on than just having talent. On the other hand, the freedom that we have, because of our politics, is extraordinary. Compared to the nineteenth century, it's amazing, and that has led to pluralism and pluralistic thinking and acceptance of many different approaches to architecture.

BI: What about the downside of all that, the visual chaos?

FG: I'm not a theoretician. I'm not Alexis de Tocqueville. I do think democracy has produced chaos, especially visual. A lot of people don't like it and yearn for nineteenth-century images, forgetting that the politics of those images were different than the democracy we love.

BI: Do you think it's a more open system for architects today than it used to be?

FG: Yes, it's a more open system. There's more variety. There's a greater chance for talent to be nurtured and grow now than there was fifty years ago. And it's something we should support. But it's very hard for me to like other people's work. I'm supportive of Thom Mayne, Daniel Libeskind, Zaha Hadid, Greg Lynn. But I don't love everything they do.

Picking buildings from the past that I like is easier than picking buildings in the present, and I think that's just human nature. I know this from the art world. When, for example, I met [the artist] Mike Kelley twenty years ago, I liked him because he was a friend of my daughters. I got to know him, and I spent time with him. I trusted that he had something going. He was doing performance art, and I didn't know what he was talking about. But I believed something would happen, and now it has happened.

So when you see the first efforts of somebody like Zaha, I'm predisposed to support her. First of all, it's rare to find a woman with that kind of presence, with a very personal point of view, and with the guts to go duke it out in a so-called man's world and prevail. Can I say I love everything she's done? I can't. But I'm just guessing that I will, like Mike Kelley. I trust her. I believe in her.

BI: And from the past?

FG: I go back to Corbusier's chapel at Ronchamp at least once a year.

BI: When did you first see it?

FG: In the fifties, when it was first done.

BI: Why do you go back?

FG: It makes me cry. It's so beautiful. It's almost perfect. It's spiritual. It does something with the site. Even though I'm not religious, it's an uplifting experience, and I know Corbusier's work well enough to know where it came from and the struggle he went through to get it there. For seven years he worked on it, and I studied all the variations he worked on.

The other place, which I haven't been back to, is La Tourette, the monastery Corb did, which is also in the south of France, near Ronchamp. It's an amazing work. He plays with the light, and it's really beautiful. I only saw it once, but it dropped me to my knees.

I know I'm in the presence of greatness when my knees go out from under me. It happened to me with the painting where they put the crown of thorns on Christ, the painting that inspired my Israeli project.

Gehry can't recall the painter's name, so we toss around names. It's not Piero della Francesca. Not da Vinci. Raphael? Titian? "No," he says. "No. No." He gets more and more frustrated.

FG: I used to have it hanging on the wall, and then they cleaned my office and took it away and I don't know where it is. Damn it. I always get mad when I get to this point thinking about it, and then I look for it and I can't find it. I can see the painting in my head.

He takes my pen and starts sketching in my notebook — "There's Christ with the thorns, and there's an arm . . ." The sketch is indecipherable to me, so I say we'll come back to it later. But he isn't about to wait for later. Jumping up, he says, "Craig Webb will know," and leaves the room. A few minutes later he returns, smiling: Hieronymus Bosch.

FG: I went to see it in London with my friend Maggie Keswick. She was dying of cancer, so maybe there was a little edge on it. We saw it in the Sainsbury Wing that Robert Venturi did at the National Gallery. I was very excited that Venturi did this great thing, because I love Venturi, love him personally. I was very happy about that and about being with Maggie. And when we walked into the gallery and saw the painting, Maggie and I, at the same moment, just dropped to our knees. I had seen the painting before, but never

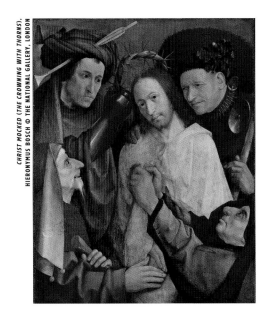

Gehry says his design for the Museum of
Tolerance in Jerusalem was influenced by
Hieronymus Bosch's painting *Christ Mocked*.

like this. The light in the gallery was just perfect that day and it was hung in the right place in the room. Everything was perfect.

Look at that painting and then at my plan for the Museum of Tolerance in Jerusalem. I'd been working on the Tolerance Museum already, so it's not like I copied it. But when you see something like that, it gives you courage somehow.

It's this thing I talk about all the time, that everything's been done before. Irving Lavin, the scholar in architecture and art at Princeton, whenever he sees my new work will say, "Well, Bernini did that . . ." Then he brings me pictures, and by God, he's usually right. It's so comforting to know that. It gives you comfort going forward, that.

Gehry stops speaking, his attention riveted by a floral arrangement at the other end of the table. He leans in conspiratorially.

FG: So where did Bernini's *Apollo and Daphne* come from? You know that sculpture? The great one, with the guy and the girl and the flowers. Look at that floral arrangement across the room.

Gehry gets to his feet and starts going through a huge pile of art books near his work-table. After a few minutes, he finds the book he's looking for and, within it, a photograph of the Bernini sculpture.

FG: Here it is. *Apollo and Daphne.* The guy was looking at nature. Bernini. He didn't come to this out of the blue. This came from something.

Gian Lorenzo Bernini, *Apollo and Daphne.* Marble statue. Galleria Borghese, Rome, Italy. Photo: Alinari/Art Resource, New York

ACKNOWLEDGMENTS

ILLUSTRATION CREDITS

INDEX

ACKNOWLEDGMENTS

I first want to thank Frank Gehry, who continually found time for our conversations despite his many other creative and professional demands. As with all his undertakings, he gave this book an enormous commitment of time and passion, not to mention patience, as I repeatedly requested one last interview, one last question. In addition to our regular interview sessions, he generously made available Gehry Partners' photo archives, his own personal archives, and his staff's time for my many inquiries and visits.

It would be difficult to imagine a better place to write this book than the Getty Research Institute, my host for many months as a guest scholar. Former GRI director Thomas Crow invited me in, and current director Thomas Gaehtgens graciously extended my stay. I am greatly indebted to so many people at the GRI, and especially to Sabine Schlosser, Martha Alfaro, and Charles Salas. I would also like to thank the GRI's Wim de Wit, Julio Sims, Jasmine Lin, Jay Gam, Donna Beckage, and particularly George Weinberg.

I am fortunate in having smart and tolerant friends who gave me excellent counsel when I needed it and solitude when that was required. I am particularly indebted to Susan Grode and Angela Rinaldi for their extraordinary gifts of time and expertise, as well as to Gayle Lewis, Laurie Becklund, Alexis Smith, Eric Lax, JoEllen Williamson, and my agent, Susan Ramer.

For their help in illuminating various Gehry projects for me or in otherwise providing me with important material, I wish to thank Abby Sher, Ultan Guilfoyle, Stephanie Barron, Ernest Fleischmann, and Thomas Krens, as well as Peter Alexander, Carl Andre, Charles Arnoldi, Giselle Artega-Johnson, Billy Al Bengston, Maria Bidaurreta, Peter Brenner, Kim Bush, Barbara Casey, Carol Casey, Antonia Coffman, Barry Diller, Jeanne Dreskin, Sidney

Felsen, Gil Garcetti, Eleanor Goldhar, Michael Govan, Robert Graham, Elizabeth Hinckley, Thomas Hines, Robert Hollister, Shannon Johnson, Jun Kanai, Jennifer Kellen, Barbara Kellner, Lyndel King, Richard Koshalek, Eric Levin, Nicole Littrean, Michael Maltzan, Jim McHugh, Keith Mendenhall, Carol Merrill-Mirsky, Lynette Nyman, Melissa Parsoff, Sydney Pollack, Piper Wynn Severance, Jason Stewart, Gwen Sutter, Joe Thiel, Juan Ignacio Vidarte, Greg Walsh, and Jessica Youn. I am also extremely grateful for the transcription skills of Victoria Kaplan and secretarial assistance from Katie Pope.

My incomparable assistant, the artist Lindsay Ljungkull Clark, helped me gather and select the two hundred pictures in this book. Besides her enviable organizing ability, computer savvy, and great spirit, Lindsay was a wonderful sounding board for the entire project. At Gehry Partners, Rhiannon Gharibeh and Laura Stella spent many hours reviewing and organizing archival images, answering inquiry after inquiry, and giving generously of their knowledge and time. Amy Achorn and Jill Konek were similarly gracious in helping to schedule and assure my countless meetings with Gehry and others. Gehry's chief of staff, Meaghan Lloyd, was invaluable as a resource, as were Gehry Partners' Edwin Chan, Berta Gehry, Dennis Shelden, and Craig Webb.

My great thanks to Jonathan Segal, my editor at Knopf, for his wise and incisive editing and for his continual enthusiasm for this project, and to his hardworking and diligent assistants, Kyle McCarthy and Joey McGarvey. I would also like to express my gratitude to Knopf's design director Peter Andersen for his early guidance, Iris Weinstein for her elegant design and collaborative spirit, Chip Kidd for his smart cover, and Ellen Feldman for her attention to detail.

As ever, I wish to thank Richard Schickel for his keen intelligence, unrivaled sense of humor, and willingness to sit through too many movies alone. Despite his own many deadlines, he always made time for advice, encouragement, and elusive adverbs.

Accademia, Florence, Italy/Scala/Art Resource, New York—90

Adoc-photos/Art Resource, New York—128

Peter Alexander Studio, Photo: Brian Forrest—54

Charles Arnoldi Studio, Photo: Jacob Melchi—xiv

Artifice Images, Photo: Earl Morsund—21

Associated Press—79

AP/Matty Zimmerman—140

Billy Al Bengston Studio, Photo: Samuel Freeman—59

Alex Berliner © Berliner Studio/BEImages—114

Professor Caroline Black Print Collection, Connecticut College—126

British Museum, London, Photo: Erich Lessing/Art Resource, New York—131

Lindsay Ljungkull Clark—16

Columbia Archives, Columbia, Maryland—52

Condé Nast Publications, Photo: Roger Dong—216

Dia Center for the Arts, New York. Art © Judd Foundation, licensed by VAGA, New York. Photo: Stewart Tyson—8

Empire Studios—15

Sidney B. Felsen—61

Galleria Borghese, Rome, Italy. Photo: Alinari/Art Resource, New York—271

Gil Garcetti—115

Frank Gehry—197

Courtesy of Frank Gehry—x, 6, 36, 161

Sam Gehry—xvii

Gehry Partners, LLP—ix, xi, xii–xiii, xvi, xviii, xix, 4, 11, 13, 15, 18, 30, 37, 49, 66, 68, 71, 72, 75, 77, 78, 82, 83, 84, 88, 89, 93, 95, 96, 106, 113, 117, 124, 129, 134, 142, 145, 146, 147, 152, 161, 166, 167, 168, 175, 181, 189, 190, 191, 192, 204, 205, 206, 208, 209, 210, 211, 214, 217, 220, 224, 226, 227, 228, 229, 231, 233, 236, 237, 238, 239, 240, 241, 242, 243, 244, 246, 247, 249, 250, 254, 261, 262, 266, 270

Fernando Gomez, Courtesy of Ultan Guilfoyle—200

Robert Graham Studio—57

The Solomon R. Guggenheim Foundation, New York, Photos: David Heald—103, 133, 139, 141, 259

Ultan Guilfoyle—82, 135, 156, 200

Lucien Herve, Research Library, Getty Research Institute, Los Angeles. Artists Rights Society (ARS), New York/ADAGP, Paris/FLC—44, 45

Hollywood Bowl Museum Collection—107

Barbara Isenberg—128

Gary Kubicek—52

Eric S. Levin—221, 222

Museum Associates/Los Angeles County Museum of Art—101, 102

Thomas Mayer/thomasmayerarchive.com—xiii, 75, 77, 154, 223

Jim McHugh—26, 51, 122

The Metropolitan Museum of Art/Art Resource, New York—144

MIT Museum—176

Issey Miyake, Photo: Paul Warchol—145

The Museum of Contemporary Art, Los Angeles. Art © Rauschenberg Estate/Licensed by VAGA, New York—60

National Gallery, London—270

Norton Simon Museum of Art, Pasadena, California—98

Sydney Pollack—147, 198, 199

Patricia A. Sampson, MIT/EECS—175, 182, 184, 185

Julius Shulman Photography Archive, Research Library, Getty Research Institute, Los Angeles—19, 27

THE SIMPSONS™ & © 2005 Twentieth Century Fox Film Corporation. All rights reserved—xvi

Tim Street-Porter—66, 119, 123

Tiffany & Co.—193, 195

Tiffany & Co., Photo: Richard Pierce—194

Coll. Marco Valsecchi, Milan, Italy. © 2008 Artists Rights Society (ARS), New York/SIAE, Rome. Photo: SCALA/Art Resource, New York—6

Michael Webb—161

Don F. Wong—71, 87, 88

Collection of the author—25, 33, 137, 158

INDEX

Page numbers in *italics* refer to illustrations.

A NOTE ABOUT THE AUTHOR

Barbara Isenberg writes and lectures about arts issues and personalities. Formerly a staff reporter for both *The Wall Street Journal* and the *Los Angeles Times,* she has also written for *Esquire, Time, Talk, The Nation, Ms.,* and London's *Sunday Times.* Her books include *Making It Big: The Diary of a Broadway Musical* and *State of the Arts: California Artists Talk About Their Work.* She received a Distinguished Artist Award from the Los Angeles Music Center and has been a Visiting Scholar at the Getty Research Institute. She lives in Los Angeles.

A NOTE ON THE TYPE

This book was set in Granjon, a type named in compliment to
Robert Granjon, a type cutter and printer active in Antwerp, Lyons,
Rome, and Paris from 1523 to 1590. Granjon, the boldest and most
original designer of his time, was one of the first to practice
the trade of typefounder apart from that of printer.
Linotype Granjon was designed by George W. Jones, who based his
drawings on a face used by Claude Garamond (ca. 1480–1561) in his
beautiful French books. Granjon more closely resembles
Garamond's own type than do any of the various
modern faces that bear his name.

COMPOSED BY

North Market Street Graphics, Lancaster, Pennsylvania

PRINTED AND BOUND BY

Tien Wah Press, Singapore

DESIGNED BY

Iris Weinstein